DEDICATION

Dedicated to the affectionate memory of
Ray and Gwyn Rogers
without whose love for the history and people of this area this
book would not have been possible. They are both sorely missed.

I would also like to make special mention of Stan, left, and
Geoff Clarke for the many happy hours spent in Gas Works
House listening to stories about "Old Stur".

Members of the Burt Family outside their house at No 3 Penny Street in 1914

Around and About
STURMINSTER NEWTON

A Photographic Journey
by Steve Case

To Mindy,
With best wishes,

Steve Case

Sturminster Newton Museum & Mill Society

The Bull Inn circa 1900. During the 1880s, on the first day of Shroton Fair (held on 25th and 26th September), a certain Steven Adams would set up a stall outside the inn offering for sale cakes and sweets. This event became known as Bridge Fair. At the rear of the Bull there used to be a slaughterhouse and an animal Pound.

Profits from the sale of this publication will be donated to Sturminster Newton Museum & Mill Society to help maintain and preserve the town's history.
Orders to:** **Sturminster Newton Museum & Mill Society, 1 Old Market Cross House, Market Cross, Sturminster Newton, Dorset DT10 1AN

First published in 2015 by Sturminster Newton Museum & Mill Society

ISBN 978-1-872270-06-7

Designed and produced by Steve Case and Penny Mountain

Printed and bound by Short Run Press Ltd, Exeter

A CIP catalogue record for this book is available from the British Library

While every care has been made to ensure the accuracy of the information in this book, the publisher cannot accept responsibility for any mistakes that may inadvertently have been included. Similarly, the publisher has made every effort to contact and acknowledge copyright holders of the illustrative material. (If they have been unsuccessful, copyright owners are invited to contact them directly.)

Introduction

The idea for this book was born out of my involvement in *STUR The Story of Sturminster Newton* (Sturminster Newton Museum & Mill Society) and *Sturminster Newton Through Time* (with Roger Guttridge, Amberley Publishing). Very different and satisfying projects, they fuelled my interest, but they also generated a huge amount of photographic material of which I was only able to use a small percentage. I always felt that the best of this additional material should be published so that people could enjoy this rich record of the history and customs of the area, and so I began this project.

Despite this wealth of material, I wondered at first how it would be possible to fill a book of this size solely with photographs; of course, by the end I wondered how I was going to fit them all in. Inevitably compromises had to be made along the way, but the final selection is, hopefully, the stronger for it.

I have tried to put names to as many people as possible in the photographs, although this has not always been straightforward. For example, one photograph, which in the end was not used in this book, featured six tradesmen whom I couldn't identify. I gave copies of the image to three people who had been around at the time, and they independently arrived at three entirely different sets of names. That is an extreme example, but even where identification has been easy, the correct spellings is almost another chapter in itself.

So many people have helped me along the way, and I have tried to credit them for their contributions overleaf. However, I would not wish to offend anyone by exclusion so here extend a general 'thank you' to all who helped in any way. This book may have my name on the cover but it only exists because of the interest and help I have received from so many people over the years, many of whom are, sadly, no longer with us.

I would also like to pay tribute to all the photographers, known and unknown, without whom these memories would simply be, well, just memories, with nothing visual to illustrate or record them. Of particular note in the early 1900s is a collection of photographs taken by the late Charlie Stride and, recording the latter part of the century, the wonderful work produced by Helmut Eckardt. I have named only two, but this area has been truly blessed with some very gifted photographers over the years.

To round off, I have to thank two people in particular, without whose support and advice this book *really* would not have been possible: Penny Mountain, for being the consummate professional in all things editorial and book layout and for being such a good friend; and, last but not least, Jo Trowbridge. Jo has put up with the months of untidiness, of piles of books and paperwork and goodness knows what else, and she has been a part of this project at every stage. I can honestly say that without her constant support and patience the book would have been a nonstarter.

So, please sit back and enjoy this photographic journey. I hope that the book gives you as much pleasure as I have had in putting it together.

Steve Case, July 2015

Acknowledgements

I would like to thank the following for their help and support during the making of this book: Pat Ager, Sue Allard, Ann Allen, Graham Allen, Kirsty Allen, Madeleine Barber, Hazel Benstead, Pat Billen, David Boulton, Alan Brown, Joan Brown, Roy Burden, Tony Butler, David Byrne, Brenda Byrne, Colin L Caddy, Gordon Chant, Jean Churchill, Mary Clacy, Stan Clarke, Geoff Clarke, Annette Clarke, Win Clarke, Pam Cole (née Snook), Judith Coombe, Audrey Cooper, Betty Cowley, Averil Cross, Alf Cuff, Barry Cuff, Mrs Dorothy Curtis, Harry Dawes, Gracie Dawes, Rev John Day, Helen Deighton, Sylvia Denham, Pat Dodson, Helmut Eckardt, Jonathan Eckardt, Paul Fiander, Mrs Eileen Fry, Roger Guttridge, Irenee Haines, Olive Hall, Alan Hammond, Vivien Hammond, Alan Hannah, Alan Harrison, Felicity Harrison, Jim Hatcher, Peggy Hatcher, J W T House, Ian Kendall, Kevin Knapp, Melanie Knapp, Betty Lane, Flossie Lane, Denise Le Voir (née Barnett), Barry Lewis, Dave Lewis, Pete Loosmore, Sarah Marsh, Michael Marshall, Pat Moody, Terry Morgan, John Morley, Derek Mountain, Penny Mountain, Linda Perrett (née Leamon), Joan Pitts, Ray Rogers, Gwyn Rogers, Andrew Rogers, Mark Rogers, Simon Rogers, Sylvia Rose, Stan Score, Margaret Score, Jacqueline Sheriff, Arthur Stockley, Sylvia Stokes, Charlie Stride, Pete Strong, Betty Tite, Arnold Trowbridge, Martin Trowbridge, Jo Trowbridge, Val Trowbridge, Muriel Tulk (née Stone), Liz Warham, Bob Weaver, Ruth White, Tania White, David Williams, Carolyn Wilson, Roy Woolridge and Jacqui Wragg.

Special thanks to the Committee of the Sturminster Newton Museum & Mill Society and for access to and use of items held in the collection of Sturminster Newton Museum.

I am especially grateful, too, to John Morley, who took many of the interesting and high quality images used in the Creamery chapter. Also to Colin L Caddy for the use of his and of J W T House's wonderfully evocative photographs of the Somerset & Dorset Railway at Sturminster Newton.

Finally, I am grateful for the support of retailers in the town and in particular to Philip Hart and Tony Butler. I would also like to express my thanks to The Exchange.

Bibliography

Roscoe, Ernest (ed), *The Marn'll Book*, Blackmore Press (1952)

Sturminster Newton Museum Society, Penny Mountain (ed), *STUR The Story of Sturminster Newton*, Dovecote Press Ltd (2006)

Guttridge, Roger, *Blackmore Vale Camera*, Dovecote Press (1991)

Whitfield, Christopher (ed), *Around the Maypole – The Shillingstone Millennium Book*, Shillingstone Parish Council (2000)

St George, Kate M (ed), *Child Okeford – A Dorset Village*, Child Okeford Millennium Book Committee (1999)

Knott, Olive, *Tales of Dorset*, The Gavin Press (1985)

Knott, Olive & Rogers, Raymond, *Pictorial History of Sturminster Newton*, Dorset Publishing Company (1973)

Smith, Graham, *Dorset Airfields in the Second World War*, Countryside Books (1999)

Hann, Maurice, *Policing Victorian Dorset*, Dorset Publishing Company (1989)

Mansel-Pleydell (ed), The Rev J C M, *Poems in the Dorset Dialect by Robert Young ("Rabin Hill")*, Dorset County Chronicle Printing Works (1910)

Senior & Godwin's Sturminster Newton Market Report for 1964

Excerpts from the Sturminster Parish Magazine from 1915 & 1917

Ibberton Village in the Year 2000 (published online at http://ibbertonvillagehall.btck.co.uk/VillageBook2000)

Contents

Right The White Hart and the
Market Cross in Sturminster Newton

Market Day

The main thoroughfare of the Market in full flow shortly before its closure.

Above The Dairy Sale Ring with a Friesian cow about to be sold by auctioneer Paul Lewis.

Below Auctioneer Paul Lewis, right, with well-known local dairy farmer Bob Tite.

Above Showing a Limousin calf with Owen Russell, right, who helped out at the Market.

Below Outside the café owned and rented out by Senior & Godwin. At one time
Mrs Upshall ran it and sold sandwiches, cakes, pasties and tea and coffee.

Looking uphill with the Market offices on the left and the Corn Exchange on the right.

Looking down towards the Rivers Arms Hotel with the Market Offices on the right.

Looking across from the Market towards the shops in Station Road.

Left Auctioneer Richard "Dickie" Burden (wearing the hat).

Below The old Rivers Arms yard where weekly auctions and monthly furniture sales took place.

Right An auction in progress at the Rivers Arms yard. No visit to Sturminster on Market Day would have been complete without a visit to Dickie Burden's auctions. He started running them in the 1970s and they continued until his death in 1991 when his son Christopher took over the business.

The late Margaret Score enjoyed telling how Dickie was once auctioning a picture of what he described as a border collie dog. A woman in the crowd declared, "That's not a border collie!" "Maybe not," said Dickie, "but it's near the edge."

Above An early photograph, taken about 1905, showing the pig market when horse-drawn wagons were still the main mode of transport.

Above A poultry and rabbit sale, again circa 1905.

Above Matthew Price of the National Farmers Union standing beside the Market Bell that now resides in pride of place above the stairway in The Exchange.

On market day Sturminster was full of interesting characters. Eli Short *above* began his working life in the Newfoundland fishing industry and in his later years became a drover. He was from Hinton St Mary and a familiar sight in Sturminster. It was said that on many occasions he had to be pushed home in a wheelbarrow, the reason for which can be seen in his left hand.

Above It wasn't only the people who were full of character at the Market, even the buildings had a look all of their own. The door to the left was the entrance to Senior & Godwin's office, the middle section was a café, in latter years run by the Red Rose, and to the right was an antique shop called Magpie's Nest.

Above and *right* This interesting object was one of the mobile buying rings used at the Market. After every sale, the buying ring would be pushed along manually by the farmers and buyers to the next pen where an animal was to be sold.

Above One of the buying rings in action with auctioneer Philip Venner.

Right This Market Report from 1964 gives a good illustration of the huge volume of livestock that passed through Sturminster Newton Market.

SENIOR & GODWIN

Chartered Auctioneers & Estate Agents

STURMINSTER NEWTON MARKET REPORT

Telephone: 244 (4 lines)

STURMINSTER NEWTON MARKET 1964

111,603 LIVESTOCK SOLD

1964 showed an all round increase of 10% throughput over the record of 1963, all sections being up in numbers; marketings and prices were generally more level than in 1963 and the year finished on a firm tone: the popularity of liveweight sales continues to grow, and an encouraging feature of 1964 was the better meat prices resulting in substantial reductions in the cost of the Guarantee Payments.

CLEAN CATTLE, 5,314, increased 11%, with a fairly level throughput; prices on average were up about 30/- per cwt, on 1963, reaching the peak around midsummer, and little difference between Spring and Autumn levels: the Autumn glut of past years has virtually disappeared, and the Guarantee Payments were negligible in the second half of the year. More cattle were marketed young, and the quality generally improved, but there is still a big unsatisfied demand for best quality beef cattle.

FAT COWS and BARRENERS - 8,292 Cows and Bulls were sold, 9% up on last year, with heavy sales in January-February due to the Continental trade, and peak prices averaging £7-£7.l0s. 0d per cwt. In May to July; best Friesian Cows continued to lead the trade. There was some recession in demand in the Autumn, but prices ended strongly.

MILK CATTLE at 4,428 were up 26%, with heavier supplies in the Autumn, and many cows from herd dispersals. Trade continued strong for all good quality milkers, but second quality sorts are not wanted. Friesians continue dominant, but latterly Ayrshires showed some recovery owing to the quality milk scheme: there was a strong Autumn demand for good Channel Island Milkers. There is a large unsatisfied demand for best milk cattle, especially Friesian Heifers.

STORE CATTLE - 3,055 sold, being an increase of 47%, good numbers coming forward in Spring and Autumn. Outwintered Beef Stores are becoming scarcer, and more young housed Beef Cattle were sold for growing on. Trade in the Spring was very fast for all Beef Stores, older Stores were easier in the Autumn, but Young Cattle maintained a strong trade. Dairy Young Stock continued to be dominated by the Friesians, which met a fast trade, many more could have been sold to advantage.

CALVES: a new record of 44,674 Calves, up 7½% on last year, over 1,000 a week being sold from the end of August to end November. The general quality of calves continues to improve, with more stronger rearers 4 to 8 weeks old. Best demand was for bull calves, the Black Hereford Crosses still leading the prices at about last year's levels, but Friesian Bulls gained ground and were up quite £2 per head, due to the Barley Beef demand. Good Friesian Heifers scarce and in stronger demand, Charollais now very few. Demand for Veal and Bobby Calves good throughout the year.

FAT PIGS, 9,705 increased 20% and a level throughput; a good pork trade throughout the year; bacon was a more even trade than in 1963 although moderate in Spring and early Summer, but ended better.

STORE PIGS, 32,259, were up 5% with rather more Strong Stores: a continuing improvement in quality was noted with a firm demand, and pig breeders generally enjoyed a better year than the fatteners.

SHEEP at 3,876 also increased 5% mainly from Spring and Summer marketings: trade for the first half year was about comparable to 1963, but better in the second half, and more Fat Lambs and Hoggets could have been sold to advantage, especially Lambs up to 44 lbs. liveweight.

Above Outside the Milk Cattle livestock auctions. This photograph was taken shortly before the Market closed, so it's not hard to imagine what the main topic of conversation would have been. It was a time of mixed emotions for many people and often for entire families.

Above A general view of the animal pens and the Calf Sale Ring.

Above An aerial view of Sturminster Newton Market taken in August 1972. The town centre is towards the top left and Bath Road travels diagonally across the top of the picture while Station Road drops down the left-hand side.

Above A view of one of the entrances to the Market off Station Road. To the right is the Corn Exchange and to the left is the old Market Office.

Above Inside the Cheese Stall: on the left is Jane House, in the middle is Joan White, and on the right is Tania White.

Left The queues for cheese on Market Day were legendary, but it was always worth the wait.

Below More of the old business units on the Market site. The Cheese Stall is at the far left.

Above A view of the inside of Senior & Godwin's Market site office. This was where much of their business was conducted on Market Day.

Above For many years there was a Women's Institute Market on Mondays; more recently this has become known as the Country Market. At present there are 12 Country Markets in Dorset; they belong to a much larger nationwide group of around 400 markets across England, Wales and the Channel Islands.

Two rare colour photographs of the Market site taken in 1964. *Top* The view from one of the old Milk Factory buildings with Station Road in the foreground, looking towards Bath Road. The brick building top right behind the pole is where Reddleman House is today.

Above The lower part of the Market site looking towards Station Road with the Creamery chimney to the right of the photograph. Hambledon Hill is in the background to the left.

Of course, no chapter on Market Day in Sturminster would be complete without mentioning the many stallholders who turn up week after week, and in some cases year after year, in all weathers, to provide such a valuable service to the town. The photographs on these two pages were taken in the 1980s.

When the closure of Sturminster Newton Market was announced, a big campaign was launched to try to save it. There followed countless meetings and discussions, and a poster campaign. The large poster above was tied to the railings of the Railway Gardens; cars went around with stickers urging people to "Support Stur Market"; the same stickers went up in shop windows around the town. Scruffy the cat presides over Petticoat Lane's window campaign *below.* The shop used to be to the right of the White Hart. Eventually, despite every effort, the Market closed in 1997.

The Town Centre

At the edge of the town centre, on the corner of Ricketts Lane and Bridge Street, lies the old Bakery. This delightful picture of Inkpen's Bakery shows Cecil and Rosina Inkpen, the children of Tom and Sarah Inkpen, and probably dates from around 1910.

Market Day in the Market Place before the purpose-built Market site was built. The photograph was taken in about 1900, from the vantage point of the old Police Station (see below). The shop at bottom right belonged to Mrs Hawkins who was a draper; later it was run by a Miss Brooks before becoming Elford's Coffee House.

An early photograph of Sturminster Newton's original Police Station. The man leaning against the railings is thought to be Sergeant Day. Above the main entrance, the words COVNTY POLICE can still be seen clearly today. Built around the late 1850s at the northern end of the Market Square, it had a commanding view of the town centre, overlooking the junction of Bath Road and Station Road. The building remained in use until about the mid-1960s when a new Police Station was built in Brinsley Close.

Above Sturminster Newton's Police Force circa 1900. *Back row from left* No 117 Constable Soloman Elsworth, No 55 Sergeant Richard Baverstock, No 5 Constable John Watts, No 86 Constable Albert Todgay and No 65 Constable Henry Barden. *Front row from left* No 105 Constable David Northover, Inspector James Collins and No 131 Constable John Hine.

Not everyone was happy to have a police station in the town. On 29th January 1861 the *Dorset County Express & Agricultural Gazette* reported the following: "Sturminster Newton. Last week some person with great violence, threw a stone through one of the windows of our new police station. The impetus was so great that it forced its way through a strong wire blind inside; but the police have not succeeded in detecting the miscreant. Such an outrage we are happy to say is exceedingly rare in our quiet town, but if it is to be repeated, it will behove the constabulary to use a little more vigilance".

Right This business card was found in the old Police Station during alterations. It harks back to a time when the site was occupied by Mitchell's Soap and Candle Factory. Every year Mr Mitchell would give a large Christmas candle to each of his customers. Local dialect poet Robert Young recounts in *Early Years* how on one occasion Mitchell's two sons made a special candle for an old cobbler and in the wick they put grains of gunpowder.

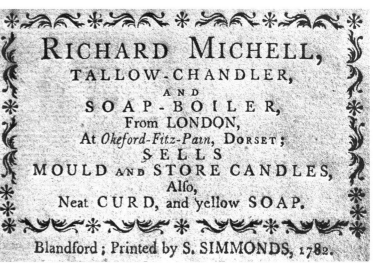

RICHARD MICHELL,
TALLOW-CHANDLER,
AND
SOAP-BOILER,
From LONDON,
At *Okeford-Fitz-Pain*, DORSET;
SELLS
MOULD AND STORE CANDLES,
Also,
Neat CURD, and yellow SOAP.

Blandford; Printed by S. SIMMONDS, 1782.

Above Market Day outside the Swan Hotel circa 1900. The Carpenters Arms public house is to the left of the Swan. In 1903 the landlord of the Swan Hotel was Frank Ford and it was then listed as a family, commercial and posting house, as well as a wine and spirit merchant, which had good accommodation for cyclists and motorists.

Above The Methodist Church's Boys Life Brigade Band prepares to lead off for a Sunday School Treat in 1909. In front are Jim Selby, Jim Northover and Sam Bracher and holding the big drum is Charlie Selby. The bareheaded man behind the drum is "Daddy" Wilkins, headmaster of the Wesleyan school. On the far right, wearing the trilby, is Charlie Cake, a grocer in Bridge Street. Sidney Charles Brickell's Fishmonger & Fruiterer's shop was in the Market Place where Marsh's is today.

Above Members of the Sturminster Newton Rifle Volunteers taken in 1892. On the far left is John Rose, aged 36, a tailor from Bridge Street, and sixth from the left is Sidney Rose, aged 22, from Fiddleford Mill.

The dialect poet Robert Young wrote about them in his poem "The Riflemen O' Blackmwore Vale" subtitled "A Song of Invasion", at the beginning of 1860. There had been a threat of invasion leading to an increase in men wanting to enrol in what was originally the Rifle Volunteers and later, in 1908, became the Territorials.

Below is an eyewitnesses account of an event featuring the group above taken from an anonymous letter held in Sturminster Newton Museum's collection:

"On one Whit Monday the local Volunteer Company were taken for a march to Binghams Melcombe about 8 miles away, the home of their Lieutenant William-Watts (afterwards Sir William).

They reached their destination and, after displaying their achievements in the art of war, they were royally entertained with the hospitality being enjoyed 'not wisely but too well'. The company was under the command of their Captain, H C Dashwood Esq who marched with them on their journey out and back. As evening drew on a crowd collected in the Market Place to greet the warriors after the fatigue of the strenuous day. I was one of that crowd.

As darkness came on a weary band of armed men toiled up the street. We were mildly appalled to see that the company had not returned in that perfection of military array which had marked their departure in the morning. On the contrary their ranks had lost that proud formation, being now broken and chaotic. A number of the company were 'under the influence' as shown by weapons borne in a manner most unmilitary and their hats worn at all angles but principally pushed to the backs of their heads for the better relief of heated brows.

The Captain appeared to be greatly scandalized by this deviation from good deportment and seemly behaviour. He halted the Company in the Market Place and addressed a short but scathing lecture to the delinquents, after which he gave the order to 'dismiss'. The Captain's gardener, William Cluett, sought to propitiate the wrath of his Commanding Officer by calling for three cheers, but in the midst of his congratulatory remarks his legs failed him and he subsided to the ground at his Master's feet.

The visit to Binghams Melcombe was not repeated."

Above Mr Slade traded from the late 1800s until around 1930 as a "Hair Dresser, Perfumer and Tobacconists". The premises later became Bryant's, also a gents hairdressers and tobacconists, and more recently Maynards, sometimes known as the Card Shop, which sold confectionery, ices, cards, stationery and fancy goods. Today, extensively modified, it is the premises of Eyes Right Opticians.

Above The Portman Hunt meets in the Market Place on 26th January 1923. The Hunt was formed in 1858 after Mr Farquharson, whose hunting territory had comprised the whole of Dorset and most of Cranbourne Chase, gave up hunting in 1856. At a meeting on 8th April 1857 at the King's Arms in Dorchester, it was decided that Dorset be divided up into separate hunts, the Portman Hunt being one of them.

Right Today's chemist's used to be the premises of Arthur Robert Hallett. He was a watch and clockmaker and jeweller who had his own business for more than 60 years. It was Mr Hallett who was responsible for installing the original clock above the shop, a version of which hangs there today.

Many of the old photographs of the town, taken in the early part of the 1900s, have the stamp of A R Hallett's on them.

Mr Hallett was a musician and the conductor of an orchestra that had up to 30 members; he also ran and conducted a military band; and he was choirmaster of the Methodist Church. At one time he was a member of the Parish and Rural Council. He re-organised the local Fire Brigade and was its captain until 1938. He was an ardent gardener, responsible for much of the planting in the Recreation Ground to which he presented the old shelter that used to overlook the river. And he was a voluntary ambulance driver.

A R Hallett was a grandson of the local Dorset dialect poet Robert Young.

Above The Sturminster Newton Orchestra at a garden party in 1911 held at Lindens, Goughs Close in Sturminster Newton. Arthur Hallett is fifth from left in the back row.
Back row from left Will Barnett, Mr Miles, Cyril Hallett, Bob Holdway, Arthur R Hallett, Fred Cowley, Percy Collins, Albert Harvey, Arthur Barnett. *Middle row from left* Mrs Arthur Hallett, Miss or Mrs Shave, Mrs Roberts, Mrs Arthur Barnett. *Front row from left* Dorothy Knott, Roy Harding, Rita Miles.

Above J & J Loader's butcher's shop in 1983 with Herbert Franklin standing in the doorway. Jim and Jill Loader retired in 2006 after trading for 36 years. The building and that on the right of the shop used to be the Crown Hotel, which closed in the early 1900s. The short section of railing which remains outside of the premises still retains its small moulded crowns, reflecting the buildings' past identity. Above Loader's were the Assembly Rooms.

Right A poster for a public meeting in the Assembly Rooms at the Crown Hotel in 1857.

Above Dancing outside Marsh's in the Market Place during the Coronation Day celebrations of 1953. Brothers Edward Bramwell Marsh and Harry William Marsh owned the garage that used to be in Station Road in about 1930 (where their store and workshop is today). In about 1940 Edward rented the premises that today is E B Marsh, from the Rivers Estate and ran both the garage and the electrical business. In the late 1940s he bought the property while Harry went on to be a builder. The front of the shop has changed gradually over the years, the most recent alteration being in 1993.

SYMPATHY

WITH THE SUFFERERS BY

THE INDIAN MUTINY !!

A PUBLIC

MEETING

WILL BE HELD

On Thursday, 19th of November, 1857,

AT TWO O'CLOCK IN THE AFTERNOON,

AT THE ASSEMBLY ROOMS,

Crown Hotel,

STURMINSTER NEWTON,

To express the sympathy of the Inhabitants thereof, and of the Neighbourhood, with the Sufferers by the Mutiny in *India*, and to raise Subscriptions in their behalf.

H. Ker Seymer, Esq., M.P.,

WILL KINDLY TAKE THE CHAIR.

THE REV. H. F. YEATMAN, L.L.B.,

And other Gentlemen, will Address the Meeting.

LADIES

Are particularly requested to attend.

Above The staff of the much-loved Hicks's store, situated where Root & Vine is today. *From left* Betty Lane, Madeline Hussey, Mary Drew, Mary Kent (who was in charge and had taken over from Doris Bennett), and Peggy Hall. Alex J Hicks was the last draper in this property, from the late 1920s to the closing down sale which started on 9th January 1984.

Above Staff of the Sturminster Newton Post Office at the PO's rear entrance in Goughs Close, probably in the late 1800s. The Sturminster Newton Post Office was situated, from 1895 to 1994, in the building to the left of Lloyds Bank. Jesse Meader, a watch and clock maker and jeweller, was the sub-postmaster. The business was later taken over by his son David Leonard Meader. In 1895 the horse and post van journeyed to Blandford, calling at Shillingstone, Sturminster and Stalbridge in the morning, picking up and delivering mail and making a return journey in the afternoon. There were three deliveries of mail a day.

Above C S Hender's premises, behind the Market Cross. Note the original town pump to the right of the picture. Charles Stephen Hender *below* ran his draper's business out of Market House from about 1901 to 1920. The 1901 census tells us that Mr Hender came originally from Bodmin in Cornwall and that he lived at Market House with his wife and son. At the time he employed two milliners and four servants, two of whom were also a drapery assistant and a drapery apprentice.

Right Mr Hender was obviously not one to miss the business opportunity presented by the death of the King.

Above Mr Short's butcher's shop on the corner of Goughs Close, now occupied by Agnes & Vera.

Above The Co-Operative Stores in 1937 decked out in celebration of the Coronation of George VI. Today this is the part of Marsh's store that overlooks the Market Cross.

Above One of the charabancs belonging to Sturminster company Sale's, owned by Mr W A Sale. The booking office, presided over by Mrs Sale, was at 3 Market Cross, now occupied by Caffé Expresso. They also sold items such as batteries and accumulators.

The heyday of the business was in the 1920s and 1930s when cars were still a luxury. At one point there were two coaches – the "Sturminster Queen", above, and the "Enterprise" – which were kept in a yard that is now the site of the car park at the top of Church Street. Mr Knott was one of the drivers and another was Jim Laws, who later did delivery driving for Strange's store, now occupied by One Stop.

It would seem that not everybody enjoyed their trips. Once, on an outing to Weymouth, one young lad couldn't be found when it was time to return home. It later turned out that he'd become so bored with the day's events that he'd decided to walk back on his own.

Above The White Hart and Knott's tailor's shop in about 1900. Note the ground level around the Market Cross compared with today. Hand-tinting black and white photographs was an art form in its own right as can be seen in other examples in this book.

Above Standing centre is fruiterer and fishmonger Mr Ronaldo Crew. When this photograph was taken in the 1920s Mr Crew was operating his business out of this building adjacent to the Market Cross. Ronaldo was born in 1885, the son of Albert and Ellen Crew who lived in Church Street (Albert was a pork butcher in Sturminster).

Below Ronaldo Crew out making his deliveries by horse and cart. He was a stalwart of the Sturminster Carnival.

Above Dousing down the fire that broke out at T W Barnett's on Thursday 26th October 1972. Taken from the White Hart, with the town's Museum on the left and Hammond's offices in the background, this photograph gives a good idea of the scale of the destruction. The store had been in the Barnett family for 145 years. At the time of the fire it was run by Squadron Leader Dennis Barnett and his wife Janet. Fortunately no one was hurt but the Barnett's lost their home and virtually all their possessions.

Above After the fire, a notice appeared on a charred doorpost: "WE WILL BE BACK SOON, Den & Janet". True to their word, they returned in this temporary portable building. Eventually a new building was erected on the site, now partly occupied by Rustic Rose, and the portable Barnett's store was taken away to begin a new life as changing rooms at Winterborne Stickland's Sports Ground.

Above Randolph Rogers standing outside his grocery and bakery shop at the top of Bridge Street in 1972. It was originally the business of James Carpenter whose nephews Francis and Randolph Rogers were apprenticed to him to learn the grocery and bakery trade. In the early days times were hard and they had little to eat. They had to untie knots in string to reuse it and made their own bags with glue and paper to package tea and sugar. They delivered as far as Mount Pleasant Farm at Woolland and to Kitford near Lower Fifehead. On the way back from their rounds they would collect dry cow pats for "fireing".

Below left Randolph Rogers serving in the shop. *Below right* A 1926 ad for Rogers' store.

F. G. & R. ROGERS,

GROCERS,

PROVISION MERCHANTS,

BAKERS & CONFECTIONERS,

Respectfully solicit your esteemed orders.

——

TRY OUR DIGESTIVE BREAD.

——

MARKET PLACE,
STURMINSTER NEWTON,

Above Sturminster Newton Museum at Market Cross.

Below Town Crier Kevin Knapp with his wife Melanie outside the Museum. Kevin is always proud to credit his wife Melanie with the creation of the sumptuous and detailed period costumes they both wear.

Re-thatching the building that is now the Museum. This was Mr Cluett's sweetshop; it used to occupy the front part of the building that faces the White Hart, and is now referred to as the "cage" as it is an open structure housing some of the Museum's external exhibits.

Sturminster Newton Creamery

The Creamery in the early 1980s, as many will remember it. This was part of the main frontage that opened onto Station Road. The distinctive Creamery chimney in the background was for many years the tallest landmark in the town. The Creamery was affectionately known by many names: the Milk Factory, the Cheese Factory or, quite simply, the Factory.

Above A typical daily scene showing how milk would have been brought to the receiving platform at the Creamery in the early days when it was still Sturminster Newton & District Farmers Ltd. The man in the trap is thought to be Bill King senior and second left on the platform, dressed in white, is Jim Ridout, grandfather of local author Roger Guttridge.

Right An early advertisement for Sturminster Newton & District Farmers Ltd.

Below When the milk was brought in to the Creamery it was weighed; the amount would determine how much the farmer would be paid.

Sturminster Newton & District Farmers

Ltd.

ENGLISH DAIRY PRODUCE

Pure Rich Cream.   Dorset Cream Butter.
BEST CHEDDAR CHEESE.

PASTEURISED MILK

Local Distributor - - MR. W. KING.

Cake, Corn & Seed Merchants

Agents and Distributors of—

A.O.M. COMPOUNDS

and

Spillers Poultry and Cattle Foods.

Motor & General Engineers

For Repairs and Overhauls to Motor Vehicles, Machinery and Plant. Churns and similar utensils made or repaired.

The Creamery, Stores and Works:
STURMINSTER NEWTON

Telephone 17

Above Analysts at the Milk Marketing Board in the late 1940s. *Standing from left* Phyllis Goddard (née Painter), Mavis Hammond (née Lewis), Joy Hatcher (née Kierle), Cicily Fish (née Parsons). *Front from left* Renee Drake (née Crips), Annie Davis (head analyst), Betty Tite (née Trowbridge).

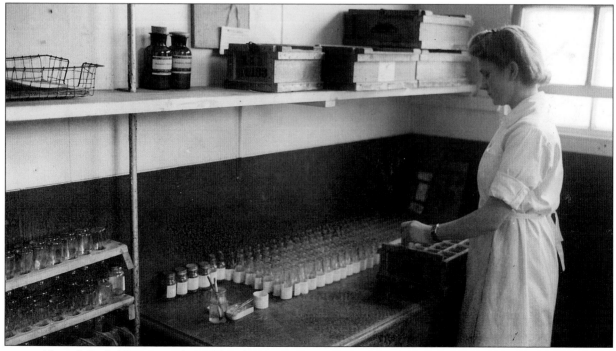

Above Mavis Hammond working in the Creamery's laboratory in the 1940s. The Creamery carried out constant checks on the incoming milk to make sure that factors such as fat levels, bacterial content and acidity were closely monitored.

Main picture A view of the outside of the Creamery in the 1950s.

Inset Alf Cuff testing whey for acidity. Whey is the watery part of milk that is separated from the curd during the cheese making process.

Above A Garner lorry belonging to Sturminster Newton & District Farmers Ltd (whose sign can be seen above the cab). On the left is its driver Frank Rose, who lived at Glue Hill, with Ernie Neakes, right. The lorry was registered to the company on 28th January 1916, and it spent its working life there. What gives the picture additional interest is that this was one of the first motor lorries to be registered in Dorset. There was little chance of driving too fast and spilling its load of milk churns as the speed was restricted to 12 miles an hour.

Above Jesse Short beside his Basingstoke-built Thornycroft J Type 40 hp flat lorry. This was also new to Sturminster Newton & District Farmers and also remained with them for its entire working life. It was first registered on 29th July 1920 and it too was restricted to 12 mph.

Above Danny Danoris making a roadside collection of milk churns from Margaret Marsh.

These two images illustrate how much the Creamery's appearance changed over the years. The photograph above was taken not long after the factory opened in 1913, whereas the photograph below, taken in the 1980s, shows the then new silos for bulk milk filling from the tankers. Today, the main building in both pictures is all that remains of the Creamery and is now the business premises of the NFU Mutual and Sturminster Dental Care.

Top left Angie Brown, Sturminster's only female cheesemaker, checking the junket before cutting it to size. Two slightly faded photographs taken circa 1970 show *top right* Phyllis Goddard cleaning the cheese before packaging, and *below left* Ernie Lloyd, one of the Cheese Graders, assessing the cheese for flavour and strength – mild, medium or mature. *Below right* "Top Hat" filling, apparently not always one of the most popular jobs – the "Top Hat" was a coloured traditional cheese coated in red wax.

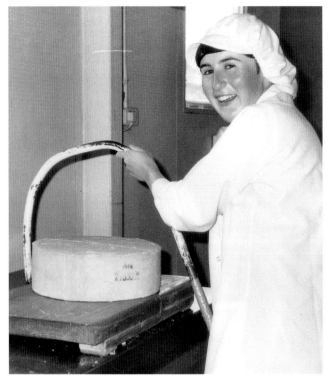

Above Catherine Lewis cutting Double Gloucester into quarters.

Left Mandy Goff cutting and packing Double Gloucester.

Below Margaret Galpin wrapping blocks of Double Gloucester.

Right Maturing cheese in storage.

In February 1978 the area suffered a heavy fall of snow and milk tankers were unable to reach their destinations. The cows were still producing milk, of course, so farmers brought it to the Creamery by any means possible. Most farmers had emergency containers for just such an occasion and Station Road saw a constant procession of tractors and other vehicles.

Above A view up Station Road with the Rivers Arms sign hanging over the road to the left.

Below Ernie Malkin, assistant manager at the Creamery, helping a farmer unload his precious cargo of milk from its container in the back of a trailer.

Above Looking down Station Road with the Rivers Arms to the right. Anything that was able to transport milk was drafted into use as can be seen from the variety of vehicles and trailers.

Below This milk tanker was used as an additional storage tank to suck out milk from plastic emergency containers. One unfortunate farmer managed to fight his way through the snow only to have his emergency container burst right at the front gates of the Creamery – all his milk was lost.

Above Curds being fed through the mill to produce chipped curds which were then pressed into cheese. On the left is Alan Parfitt and on the right Brian Cox.

Right When modern technology was introduced to the Creamery these massive blockformers replaced the manual process. Milled curds would be fed into the top and compressed into 40lb blocks of cheese under their own weight.

Below Roger Williams, surrounded by cheese moulds in the press room, trimming off the surplus dressing from a 27 kilogram cheddar.

Two views inside the Creamery circa 1992.
Above In the background are *from left* John Palin, Kevin Knapp, Phil Stainer, David Male and Nigel Busby. In the foreground, cutting the cheese for cheddaring, part of the process to producing the final cheese, are Chris Biggs and Richard Goddard.

Below, from left Robert Gardner, Nigel Busby, David Male, Richard Goddard, Phil Stainer, Ken Platt (cheesemaker), Kevin Knapp, Chris Biggs, John Palin, John Winfield, Roger Williams and Alf Cuff (cheesemaker).

Some of the many trophies and certificates awarded to the Creamery over the years.
Above Awards presented to the Creamery in 1990; and *below* awards from 1985 and 1986.

It is hard to believe that, despite all the expensive modernisations that were carried out to the Creamery, including this new whey tank in 1994, the Creamery was brought to an abrupt and premature end in 2000. In the background you can see part of the old Sturminster Newton Market that is now the site of today's Exchange.

Around the Town

Above inset Something you don't see every day – an elephant in the River Stour, just below Sturminster Bridge circa 1900. *Main picture* Taken around the same time in Sturminster. The town used to be visited by travelling street fairs of one kind or another. Among them was one known as The Happy Family, "a melancholy collection of cats, dogs, mice, rats, sparrows, and rabbits all huddled together in a large cage mounted on a truck and all looking supremely miserable, as well they might". Of greater attraction still was Wombwell's Menagerie, which featured real lions, tigers, bears, elephants and camels, along with smaller creatures such as monkeys and birds.

Above It is hard to imagine that, once, there were so many bakers in the area they had their own association. Here is the Sturminster Newton & District Baker's Association circa 1900. *Back row from left* Mr J King, Mr E Coombs, Mr J Harvey, Mr Tom Inkpen, Mr Geo Ross, Mr W Dewfall, Mr H Plowman. *Middle row from left* Mr C Burge (vice president), Mr S G Carter (hon sec), Mr W Mogg (president), Mr H Dike (ex-president), Mr T Elsworth. *Front row from left* Mr W Rose, Mr Fudge, Mrs Carter, Mrs Mogg, unknown child, Mrs Dike, Mr Gray and Mr S Burden.

Above Outside Marschall's Café in Bridge Street circa 1965 with *from left* Jim Dyke on the bicycle, Ralf Marschall, Paul Fiander, Erica Marschall and Ian Short on the motorbike. More recently this was Mr Tribes' clock shop and before that it was two businesses run side by side run by Mr Marschall: on the right was the Blue Diamond Milk Bar, and on the left was the Fish Bar. Before that it was Hendbest's Fish and Chip shop and further back again it was the workshop of one of Sturminster's most revered craftsmen, William Westcott, who created many of the decorative wooden carvings in St Mary's church.

Bridge Street used to be home to a variety of different businesses. *Above* Many will remember when Hanks, to the left of this photograph, taken in 1978, was in the Clock House. Hanks was a children's paradise for toys but they also sold stationery, birthday cards and fancy goods as well as carrying out watch, clock and jewellery repairs. To the right of Hanks at the junction with Ricketts Lane, used to be the much-missed England's bakery.

Across the road from Hanks was Coleman's *below*, which again many people may still recall, here in 1982. The shop sold sports, travel and leather goods; they also offered dry cleaning and shoe repairs, and even gave Green Shield stamps. Although some may remember Coleman's, I wonder how many will remember Tallants *right* which took over the shop afterwards; this picture dates from 1983.

Above The Reverend C H Gould surrounded by members of the Sturminster Branch of the Church Lads Brigade that he formed. Rev Gould was the local curate and known as "Passon". Among many other activities, he set up a bugle band, which would march through town with "Passon" at its head to the Sunday afternoon service at the Parish church. The service was affectionately referred to as PSA – Pleasant Sunday Afternoons. The Sturminster Town Band would also turn up and the services were always well supported.

Below The certificate issued to Edwin Rose on his admission into the Church Lads Brigade.

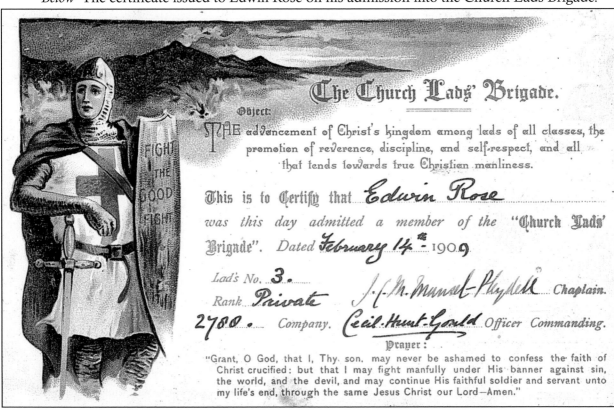

Above A print of St Mary's Church from a lithograph prepared by Hollway & Son of Bath from an original image by W C Colbourne, published by local printer W Trite in 1855.

Above St Mary's Church Choir in 1965. *Back row from left* Keith Drew, Richard Harding, Paul Finnerty, Peter Cowley, Martin Harvey, Richard Williams, Rodney Finnemore, Kevin Ricketts, Jimmy Mason, James Fish. *Third row from left* Alan Hannah (choirmaster), Graham Horne, Andrew Rogers, Keith Ricketts, Christopher Harding, Edward Pope, Jeremy Barnett, Geoffrey Clarke, Keith Goddard, Roger Guttridge, Paul Hart, John Fish, Peter Lovell. *Second row from left* Francis Musto, David Welch, Alaister James, John Matthews, Neil Fulford, Martin Stainer, John Cowley, Mark Rogers, Alan Lydford, Paul Welch. *Front row from left* Ray Rogers, Joyce Gurney, Mrs Ann Allen, Mrs Drake, Mrs Gay, Mrs Gas, Miss Bower, Miss Sutherland, Mr Miller, and Peter Clark (organist).

Above For many years the town's printing needs were fulfilled by Reg Clarke, seen here standing in the doorway of the printers at No 2 Penny Street in around 1980. On the left is Mrs Josie Card, whose family lived in the house in Penny Street pictured below (see story on opposite page).

Despite much research, the origins of this photograph are still unknown. However, I have included it as, apart from being such an unusual picture, it was in the collection of the late Ray Rogers, who preserved so many images and items relating to the town and to local life.

In 1973 Ray produced *Pictorial History of Sturminster Newton*, in association with local writer Olive Knott. The book included a story about the "Dancing Bears". The town had many visiting fairs and attractions, one of them was the appearance from time to time of two Russians with three bears. The event caused intense excitement. The bears were chained together and led through the streets by their keepers, one of whom carried a long pole with which he guided the animals as they performed. They seemed to be controlled by a strange monotonous singing from the Russians, with phrases such as "Olli olli um pum poy" and "Arum Barum, bum bum bee". This would send the poor animals shuffling around, apparently hypnotised by the sound, and they would keep dancing until the singing stopped. They performed other tricks to order.

Opposite bottom left The old Dame School in Penny Street, now No 3 Lane Fox Terrace, where Dorset poet William Barnes was taught. At one time it belonged to a cooper (a maker and repairer of barrels), who used to let the Russians and their bears stay in the outhouse (since demolished) that can be seen to the right of the photograph. The story goes that on one occasion a friend of the cooper, who also used the outhouse now and then, went in to shelter from a thunderstorm when suddenly, through the open door, a flash of lightning revealed the forms of three sleeping bears and two men. Needless to say the man beat a hasty retreat.

Above The town sign at the bottom of Bridge Street, with Beech House in the background, in 2010. The sign consists of two separate coats of arms: the yellow cross on a red background is the coat of arms of the French town, Montebourg; on the right with a green background, is the coat of arms of Sturminster Newton. The town was twinned with Montebourg in 1994 and the event was recognised by incorporating the two coats of arms into one design.

Below Church Street 2010, and Carolyn Wilson, one of our intrepid postmen and women, carries on the tradition of delivering the post regardless of the weather.

Above Strange's Grocery Store in Station Road in the late 1950s, where One Stop is today. *From left* Ray Crew, Stan Rose, Norman Upshall, Jimmy Loader, Charlie Wills, Louis Tite, Roy Hatcher, Margaret Joyce, Bill Allen (at back), Joe Horder, Barbara Spicer, Barbara Hill, Robin Strange and Billy Wills.

Below This fascinating glimpse into times past shows the provisions counter inside Strange's store in 1939.

Above Local officials and members of the Sturminster Newton Fire Brigade circa 1965.
Back row standing from left Geoff Peck, Ivor Parsons, Victor Gass, Barry Clarke, Bob (Robert) Rumbold, Terry Goddard, Steve Goddard, Jimmy Kendall, Wilf Miles, Reg Clarke, Bert Myall, Walter Ellis, Ron Goddard, Robert Newman (in front), Barry Newman (standing behind), Eddie Peck, Freddie Gray, Mr Vickers (sub officer), Joseph Holder, Jack Gass, Frank Stainer, Maurice Miller, Johnnie Peck, W Drew, Stan Warren, Fred Clarke. *Front row from left* Bert Hammond, Jim Hammond, George Northover, Bill (William) Welch, R Foster Clarke, Harry Peck (station officer), Colonel Lee Evans, Bill (William) Short, Bernard Short, "Jeddy" King and George Cluett.

Main picture The fire that destroyed the furniture factory at Butts Pond in the early 1990s.

Above Back to a time when most people had their milk delivered to their house – and in glass bottles. Here, in about 1980, Norman Upshall delivers milk in Rixon. He is standing outside the house where Annie Fudge used to live. Annie Fudge was known locally as "Annie Hoss Tird" as she used to pick up horse dung and dry it to use as fuel.

Below The cottages on the left are still there but this is how Butts Pond looked before the removal of the ash tree and the widening of the road, believed to have been in 1958.

Above A hand-tinted photograph of Sturminster Castle circa 1900 (would-be visitors should note that the ruin stands on private property).

Above Castle Farm in the early 1900s with Mr Russell, left, leaning rather casually against a dangerous-looking scythe. To the right, Dulcie and Mrs Russell.

Above Members of The Hardy Players in the Castle Grounds (part of the Castle can be made out in the background) on 9th June 1921, when they performed "Scenes From Mr Thomas Hardy's Novels", *Far from the Madding Crowd* and *Under the Greenwood Tree*, in aid of the Comrades Hut Fund for the British Legion.

Below A copy of the programme produced for the event, which Thomas Hardy himself attended along with his wife Florence.

'Bathsheba Everdene and her Lovers.'

Adapted from the famous Novel, " Far from the Madding Crowd,"
(by kind permission of the Author, Mr. THOMAS HARDY, O.M.)
Presented by the

HARDY PLAYERS.

❦❦❦❦❦

Characters :

Bathsheba Everdene	...	Miss GERTRUDE BUGLER
Gabriel Oak ...	...	Mr. T. POUNCY
Farmer Boldwood	...	Mr. H. A. MARTIN
Sergeant Troy ...	...	Mr. E. J. STEVENS
Cainey Ball } Jan Coggan }	...	Mr. T. H. TILLEY
Joseph Poorgrass	...	Mr. T. POUNCY

❦❦❦❦❦

THE FIRST LOVER.

Bathsheba and Gabriel Oak at Norcombe Farm, near Beaminster, followed by a short scene between Gabriel Oak and Cainey Ball.

❦❦❦❦

THE SECOND LOVER.

Bathsheba and Farmer Boldwood, now at Weatherbury (about six months later), followed by a humorous duologue between Jan Coggan and Joseph Poorgrass

❦❦❦❦

THE THIRD LOVER.

Bathsheba and Sergeant Troy
(a few weeks later).

❦❦❦❦

THE CONSTANT FIRST LOVER.

Bathsheba and Gabriel Oak
(about eighteen months later)

❦❦❦❦

A short explanatory introduction (prepared by Mr. Harry Pouncy) and the original verses (written for the occasion) will be read before each episode.

❦❦❦❦❦

INTERVAL.

"An Old-time Rustic Wedding,"

From the famous Novel, " Under the Greenwood Tree "
(by kind permission of the Author, Mr. THOMAS HARDY, O.M.)

❦❦❦❦

SCENE : The Green in front of Mr. Geoffery Day's Cottage in Yalbury Wood.

Introducing Old Songs and the following Country Dances, as danced in Mellstock about 1840 :—" Haste to the Wedding," " The Triumph," " The College Hornpipe," and " Five-handed Reel."

❦❦❦❦

Characters :

Reuben Dewy (the Tranter or Carrier)		Mr. W. R. BAWLER
Dick Dewy (his son) ...	...	Mr. E. J. STEVENS
Geoffrey Day (Head Keeper at Yalbury Wood)		Mr. A. C. COX
Robert Penny (a Cobbler)	...	Mr. J. KENISTON
Michael Mail (a Publican)	...	Mr. H. W. PERHAM
Joseph Bowman (a Blacksmith)	...	Mr. A. H. BUGLER
Thomas Leaf (A " Simple " Village Lad)		Mr. T. H. TILLEY
Grandfer William (the Oldest Member)		Mr. T. POUNCY
Elias Spinks (the Parish Clerk)	...	Mr. A. D. WRIGHT
Natt Callcome (the Best Man)	...	Mr. H. A. MARTIN
Enock (the Keeper's Man)	...	Mr. A. H. DAVEY
Fancy Day (Daughter of Geoffrey Day)		Miss GERTRUDE BUGLER
Mrs. Dewy (the Carrier's Wife)	...	Mrs. MAJOR
Mrs. Penny (the Cobbler's Wife)	...	Miss E. BUGLER
Susie Dewy (the Carrier's Daughter)		Miss G. EVANS
Mrs. Crumpler } Lizzie } Guests	...	{ Miss M. DAWES { Miss V. STEVENS

Above Another hand-tinted postcard: Sturminster Mill, clearly showing one of the original two waterwheels that were eventually replaced by a turbine in 1904.

Above The steering group of the book *STUR The Story of Sturminster Newton* in a publicity shot in front of the Mill in 2006. *From left* Penny Mountain (editor of *STUR*), Pete Loosmore, Pat Ager, Margaret Score and Steve Case (author of this book), and last but not least, Maisie the terrier. The steering group was just the small tip of a very large iceberg of people who spent an incredible amount of time and effort in researching the different aspects of the town's history.

Above The Mill is a magical building in a most beautiful setting. The jewel in Sturminster Newton's crown, it attracts many visitors every year. It has been photographed so many times that it's difficult to find a fresh image, but on a morning in January 2009, following a hoarfrost, I saw this scene as I was driving to work. I rushed back home, grabbed my camera and was fortunate to get this wintry shot.

Right The downside to working in the Mill is that from time to time it floods, as miller Pete Loosmore is experiencing, and certainly not for the first time.

Above The staff at Sturminster Newton High School in September 1976. *Back row from left* Mike English, Mervyn Frampton, Donald Hall, John Trevett, Terry Warder, Crichton Casbon, Peter Glen, Norman Damerell, Don Middlemore. *Front row from left* Helen Nicholson, Virginia DuFell, Di Foot, Rachel Eaton, Margaret Warham, Ian Russell, Alan Rigg, Bea Sawyer, Mary Andrews and Connie Guttridge. Missing from the photograph are Alan Newton, John Musto, Harry James, Mrs Broadhurst and Mrs Brenda Baker.

Above William Barnes School 1965/66. *Back row from left* Brian Martin, Christopher Morris, Roger Lane, Leon Dodson, David Caddy, Duncan Philips, Peter Chatfield, John Dorrington, Martin Stainer, Fred Grinnell (teacher). *Third row from left* Eamonn Helvin, Janet White, Shirley Upshall, Helen Rumbold, Francis Goddard, Sandra Ricketts, Deborah Whillet, Jean Guy, Nicola Notley, Annette Clarke, Elizabeth Hussey, Peter Cowley. *Second row from left* Zoe Cluett, Rosalind Wareham, Edith Potter, Janice Squires, Frances Haskett, Gillian Clarke, Susan Stockley, Ruth Buchan, Julie Blandamer, Karine Fulford. *Front four from left* David Welch, John Matthews, David Gale and Alaister James.

Above The elegantly posed staff of the girls and infants school (later called the Parish Room) in 1908. *Back row from left* Mrs Elkins, Mrs Drew and Miss Drew. *Front row from left* Mrs L Clarke, Miss Bugler and Miss M Rose. Mrs Drew was appointed headmistress in May 1904 and Maggie Rose was appointed headmistress in 1911. The photograph was taken by E Goodfellow who had premises in the Market Place in Sturminster as well as in Wincanton.

Above Keepers Cottage in Piddles Wood, formerly the house of the gamekeeper. The last gamekeeper recorded as living there, between 1865 and 1895, was John Swaine. The house continued to be occupied until the building was razed to the ground in the 1950s – there is no trace of it today. The last inhabitants were Mr and Mrs Dymond and their daughter Vera.

Below The Broad Oak Band circa 1900. Although this photograph has been published before, a good image is always worth another airing. *Back row from left* Jack Elkins, Frank Topp, Sam Elkins, John Short, Hedley Cluett, Ned Elkins, Tommy Tuck, Jim Short, Tom Elkins. *Front row from left* Ned Short, Arthur Moore, Bob Elkins, John Wheeler. John Wheeler (full name Henry John Wheeler), was a blind musician who had originally come from Okeford Fitzpaine. At the time of this photograph it is thought that he lived in Church Street with his parents; his father had been a tailor.

Above Sometimes the river bites back. This was the scene at the bottom of Bridge Street on the morning of 24th December 2013. Cars had been abandoned to their fate; the traffic lights continued to function but to no purpose. Not infrequently the River Stour bursts its banks after heavy rain, but for it to pour onto the main road with such force is a very rare occurrence.

Above In summer 2011 Dorset Country Council carried out extensive repairs to Sturminster Bridge. The workmen used traditional techniques to replace and rebuild the stonework, and re-pointed where necessary. Other structural repairs were carried out at the same time. It was a fascinating project to watch because the River Stour had to be partially dammed at each section so that the workforce could work safely and in the dry. Since the bridge is a Scheduled Ancient Monument all of the work was subject to approval by English Heritage.

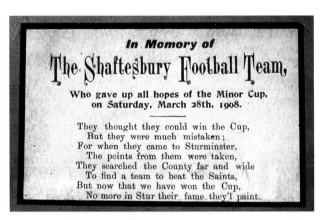

Above Sturminster Newton 1st XI in 1969. *Back row from left* Dennis Young, Geoff Eavis (trainer), John Warren, Derek Fowles, Mike Murphy, Danny Hollex, John Fish, Pete Stockley, Derek Young, Richard Shepard (chairman). *Front row from left* Jimmy Mason, Pete Hawkins, Dave Collis, Ian Trowbridge, John Francis, Arthur Stockley and Keith Dring. There was also a reserve team.

Left Sport is usually about competition, but in 1908, having beaten Shaftesbury in a home game, Sturminster went a little over the top and produced these cards "In Memory of The Shaftesbury Football Team", with a little poem just to rub it in.

In Memory of
The Shaftesbury Football Team,
Who gave up all hopes of the Minor Cup,
on Saturday, March 28th, 1908.

They thought they could win the Cup,
But they were much mistaken;
For when they came to Sturminster,
The points from them were taken,
They searched the County far and wide
To find a team to beat the Saints,
But now that we have won the Cup,
No more in Stur their fame they'l paint.

Above Sturminster Newton Football Club in 1963. *Back row from left* Albert Rose, Derek Fowles, Ken House, T Elsworth, Ken Stainer, Eddie Higgins, Pat Ridout, Les Parsons, Merv Frampton, Ernie Gorge, Bert Hammond. *Front row from left* David Rose, Dave Collis, Herbie Short, Theo Warren, Bobby Toms, Ian Trowbridge and Frank Porter.

Above This rustic cottage, in a view looking towards Lydlinch, used to stand on the main road out of Sturminster just beyond Newton. The photograph was taken in 1966 just before road widening took place, at which point the building was demolished.

Below The old Red Lion public house at Newton on the A357 in 1975 after the front porch, topped with its effigy of a Red Lion, had been in a disagreement with a passing lorry. The porch was later replaced and the lion as well, with a hollow-bodied replica. It is now a privately-owned house.

Sturminster Newton.

LICENSED PURSUANT TO ACT OF PARLIAMENT.

UNDER THE DISTINGUISHED PATRONAGE OF

THE RIGHT HON. LORD RIVERS,
THE HON. W. H. B. PORTMAN, M.P.,
THE RIGHT HON. LORD RICHARD D'AQUILA GROSVENOR, M.P.,
H. GERARD STURT, ESQ., M.P.,

JOHN HUSSEY, Esq.,	MERTHYR GUEST, Esq.,	CARR S. GLYN, Esq.,
CAPTAIN HANHAM, R.N.,	MONTAGUE GUEST, Esq., M.P.,	W. W. CONNOP, Esq.,
E. C. KER SEYMER, Esq.,	H. S. BOWER, Esq.,	R. R. HARVEY, Esq.,
M. S. YEATMAN, Esq.,	LIEUT. COL. GLOSSOP,	H. C. DASHWOOD, Esq.
	R. S. FREAME, Esq., &c., &c.,	

FIRST PERFORMANCE OF THE TENTH SEASON.

The Members of the

STURMINSTER DRAMATIC SOCIETY,

Have pleasure in announcing that they will give Two Entertainments on the Evenings of

TUESDAY, DECEMBER 30th, 1873, and
FRIDAY, JANUARY 2nd, 1874.

The Performance will commence on each Evening with the Modern Comedy in One Act entitled

THE BONNIE FISH-WIFE,

BY CHARLES SELBY.

CHARACTERS :—

SIR HICCORY HEARTYCHEER (a steady old Gentleman).................................. MR. CHEESEMAN.
MR. WILDOATS HEARTYCHEER his Son (a flighty young Gentleman) .... MR. W. C. NORMAN
GAITERS Valet to Mr. Wildoats Heartycheer (a cool Gentleman)....................... MR. MARSHALLSAY.
Miss THISTLEDOWN (a romantic young Lady)...... MISS LAVINIA ROGERS.
MAGGY MACFARLINE (a Newhaven Fish Wife, with the popular Scotch Ballad "Caller Herring ") MISS L. ROGERS.

To be followed by the Laughable Farce in One Act

Up for the Cattle Show,

By HENRY LEMON.

CHARACTERS :—

GABRIEL MARLOW (a Lawyer) .... MR. TAYLOR.
JOHN LINTON (his Clerk) .... MR. F. WILTSHIRE.
PAUL GRANVILLE... MR. R. ROSE.
PETER STROLLOP.. MR. KELWAY.
CECELIA MARLOW (Marlow's Daughter) .... MISS CLARA ROGERS.
PHŒBE BINGLEY....................... MISS LAVINIA ROGERS.

To conclude on both Evenings with the Comic Dramatic Sketch of

THE SMOKED MISER,

Above Sturminster Newton Amateur Dramatic Society's "Rosebud Ballet" junior chorus in a production of "Beauty and the Beast" in the old Hall in February 1973. *From left* Ann Faulkner (Jack Frost), Rachel Peirce, Tracy Vining, Marie Heanes (Rose Fairy), Tracey King, Catherine Taylor and Phillipa Lewis (Sunbeam Fairy).

Left Probably the earliest poster to have survived from a performance in 1873/74 of what was then Sturminster Dramatic Society. Over the years the Society has done a huge amount for the community and it continues to raise funds and provide the town with enjoyment to this day.

Above The cast of SNADS's 1983 production of "Dick Whittington". *Back row from left* Clive Gray, Chris Taylor, Jenny Powell, Robert Cowley, Andrew Davis, Peter Cowley. *Middle row from left* Ray Rogers, Gill Martin, David Cake, Dick Welsby, Marie Cole, Glenda English, Trevor Puckett, Linda Flynn, Diana Gray, Tony Brewer (wearing crown), Queenie Gibbs (in front of Tony Brewer), May Short, John Pruden. *Front row from left* Kirsty Allen, Lorraine Streeter, Emma Smith, Lisa Flynn, Tracey Vining, Bridget Rose and Lesley Allen.

Above The 1st Sturminster Newton Brownie Pack in 1961 in the Brownie Garden at the far end of the Recreation Ground overlooking the River Stour. *Adults back left and right* Gracie Dawes (Brown Owl), Jean Mathieson (Tawny Owl). *Back row from left* Jill Weeks (holding fork), Rosemary Green, Carolyn (Flo) West, Marion Moore, Marcia Pope, Judith Ridout, Liz Warham, Yvonne Lewis, Christine Tite, Hazel Stockley, Avril Russell, Noreen Martin (holding fork), Christine Hall, Janet Peck. *Front row from left* Patricia Aldwell, Jenny Matthews, Vivien Hammond, Jenny Rose, Rosemary Aldwell, Ann Weeks, Wendy Haskett, Carol Russell, Elizabeth Green and Wendy Mathieson.

Above The Sturminster Newton Cubs in the Recreation Ground in 1962. *Back row from left* Arthur Burden (Scout leader), Kelvin Ricketts, Stephen Burden, Gerald Puckett, John Ridout, Peter Robinson, Geoffrey Clarke, Jim Piper, Martin Yeatman, Dennis Martin, Chris Andrew (assistant). *Middle row from left* Peter Cowley, Keith Drew, Richard Williams, John Hatcher, Paul Yeatman, Michael Selby, Martin Clarke, Alan Knott, Peter Yeatman, . *Front row from left* Clive Weeks, Damien Bittner, Robert Hatcher, ?, Steven Chapman, Brian Martin, David Welch and Mark Rogers.

Above A view of the Market Cross area in 1962 showing the Carnival Queen and her attendants aboard their float. *From left* Christine Wilds, Carnival Queen Ann Allen and Helen Porter. The float is decorated with the then new insignia of the Rural District of Sturminster Newton, which was granted on 24th May 1962 at the old Council Offices in Bath Road.

Above A huge number of people used to turn out for the River Sports and Tug of War during Sturminster Newton's Carnival. Cars were parked all the way up Newton Hill (top right). The cottages in the background were demolished in the early 1970s. This photograph was probably taken in the 1960s.

Above The Carnival Queen selection evening on 23rd May 1980 in, of all places, the old Cattle Market. The entrants *from left* Jo Sheppard, Fennela (Fenny) Greenfield, Tania Curtis, Helen Trowbridge, Debbie Kendall, Diane Smith, Suzanna Hayward, Dana Fudge, Kim Doggerel, Jo Trowbridge, Mary Ann Short, Heather Pearson, Brenda Clothier. The winners were: 1st Jo Sheppard, 2nd Fenny Greenfield, 3rd Heather Pearson.

Above We end this chapter as we began it, with another unusual visitor. Caroline, an 8-year-old camel from Longleat Wildlife Park, made a guest appearance at the 1976 Carnival. During the day, any youngster who felt up to the challenge could have a ride, while in the evening the camel strode along in the procession. Here, on top of the camel, is former Carnival Queen Sara Tite, and many will remember Mary Kent, smiling in the foreground.

There were only 44 floats in the procession in 1976, 10 fewer than the previous year's record but still one of the best entries in years.

The Somerset and Dorset Railway at Sturminster Newton

A rare colour photograph, taken late 1964, of GWR pannier locomotive 4631 about to cross the River Stour at Sturminster Newton over Bridge No 171, on its way towards Stalbridge. This engine was shedded at Templecombe between May 1964 and February 1965. Just visible to the left of the image is a group of runners taking part in one of the Sturminster Newton High School cross-country races. The mud under the arches probably still contains the remains of plimsolls that were regularly lost in the mire during the race.

Above This beautiful winter scene with a train crossing the River Stour on its way to Stalbridge, was taken from Bonslea House, from where at one time the photographic business of Camera Technique operated.

Left Sturminster station looking towards the shops in Station Road (background right). Note the "USE GAS" sign on the building behind the station; the Gas Works used to extend from Penny Street across to Station Road.

Below Staff at Sturminster Newton Station circa 1930. *Back row from left* Bill Vincent, "Happy" Clark, Bill Stacks, Joe Marsh, Walt Fudge, Mr Moore. *Front row from left* Arthur Pope, Percy Lydford, Elsie Clarke, Bill Lush, Henry Upshall and Jack Inkpen.

Above A Standard Class 4 4-6-0 No. 75072 approaching the signal box at the eastern end of the up platform at Sturminster Newton. Four of these engines were fitted with double blastpipes and chimneys to improve draughting, which provided them with the additional power they needed to work on the S&D.

Above A Standard Class 5 4-6-0, No 73052 about to leave Sturminster Newton station on its way to Shillingstone. This engine operated regularly on the S&D.

For many years trains entering the railway cutting on the Stalbridge side of Sturminster Newton station suffered delays from the occasional landslide.

This photograph – taken about 1908 from the bridge on Bath Road looking towards the River Stour – shows workmen about to start construction of a series of brick arches into the embankment which, when completed, shored up the steep sides of the cutting and prevented further landslides. The brick arches still remain, but they are buried beneath the piles of rubble used to fill in the cutting after the closure of the railway.

Above This view of Sturminster station, looking towards Station Road in the background, shows the pronounced dip in the up platform that led to the level crossing.

Left A stunning mirrored image showing West Country No 34006 *Bude* leading Battle of Britain No 34057 *Biggin Hill* about to cross the River Stour towards Sturminster on 5th March 1966.

Below An Ivatt Class 2 2-6-2 tank, nicknamed "Mickey Mouse", arriving from Stalbridge. The white building that can just be seen centre left above the carriages is now the home of Streeters Carpets & Beds Ltd. Once the site of agricultural merchants Blandford & Webb, it was designed to support 200 tons of stored grain.

Above from left William Porter, Tommy Warren and Walt Hatcher standing in a wagon at one of the Sturminster station sidings. Note the old Creamery chimney at back left.

Main picture Standard Black 5 5056 travelling towards Sturminster Newton from Fiddleford with Hambledon Hill just visible in the background. This is now part of the North Dorset Trailway.

Above Engine 563 is a 2P 4-4-0 and was a Midland locomotive. Here, it is emerging from Bridge No 173 having come from Stalbridge.

Below The same view taken in the late 1970s. Bridge No 173, to the right of the photo, is by this stage partly filled in as construction gets under way of a new car park, which these days is the main car park serving the town. Once again, the common denominator in both images is the view of the shops in Station Road in the background.

Above On its way from Sturminster station to Stalbridge, Engine 601, a rebuilt Fowler 2P 4-4-0 with an extended fire box.

Below The cutting being filled in circa 1980, taken from Bath Road and looking towards Station Road with the white building of Streeters Carpets & Beds Ltd in the background.

Left A different and much later view of the cutting seen above and below on this page. After the railway closed the line was left abandoned for nature to reclaim. Looking towards Stalbridge with the site of the old station behind you, the bridge in the background is No 172, which was in Bath Road, and, in the foreground, Bridge No 173, which was in Station Road. The area between the two bridges was filled in and is now the site of the Railway Gardens. It was a magical place and many a child made their camp in the old cutting, myself included.

Above This is believed to have been taken by local photographer Charlie Stride near Gain's Cross at Shillingstone. The train would have passed through Sturminster and just left Shillingstone Station on its way to Blandford.

Above William Henry Owen, middle front row, was station master at Sturminster Newton for more than 41 years until he resigned due to ill health.

This framed, beautifully hand-written and illuminated address was presented on 27th November 1921 to William Henry Owen for his "duties as Station-Master at Sturminster Newton for a period of over 41 years".

It begins: "We, the Subscribers, resident in this parish, and in the surrounding and outlying towns and districts, desire your acceptance of this Illuminated Address and the accompanying cheque for Sixty Guineas on the occasion of your retirement."

On the back of the frame is a list of the 143 subscribers, detailing the individuals and professional institutions that contributed to it. This exquisite piece of craftsmanship is now in the care of Sturminster Newton Museum and is well worth seeing.

Above When the S&D line was about to close many locals went out armed with their cameras to record their own memories of the old railway. Seen here standing in front of one of the main station signs are Miss Armstrong, left, and Valerie Wallis. One of the station signs has been preserved and can be seen at the Sturminster Newton Museum.

Above West Country No 34006 *Bude* was used on one of the last "specials" to run on the S&D. Here, it has come up from Branksome on its way to Templecombe before making a return journey through Sturminster. Taken on 5th March 1966.

Not long after the Somerset & Dorset line closed anything of value was removed. These two photographs were taken during the removal of Bridge No 171 over the River Stour. The blue engine below is a Hudswell-Clarke.

Very little remains of the Somerset & Dorset Railway although the arches of Bridge No 171 still survive beside the River Stour as a lasting monument to its route through Sturminster. Another important and well-used legacy is the North Dorset Trailway, which mainly follows the line of the old S&D from Sturminster Newton to Blandford.

Election Time

Electioneering in North Dorset was a vibrant business in the early part of the 20th century, as will be seen from the following pages. It seems hard to believe today that general elections generated such enthusiasm as to bring out people in huge numbers to be part of the process. In 1905 it was thought that the turnout of voters would be encouraged by the "brilliant weather, roads hardened by the frost, an adequate supply of motor-cars, and, as the candidates say, the stimulus of a cause worth fighting for".
Above a poster for the Liberal candidate.

The two main political adversaries in North Dorset in the early 1900s: *above left* Sir Randolph Baker of the Conservative Party and a county magistrate; and *right* Arthur Walters Wills of the Liberal Party. According to one newspaper in 1905, "In the Shaftesbury district, where the people talk as quaintly as the characters in a Hardy novel, the antialien cry has made some impression." It went on to say how posters supporting Sir Randolf Baker stigmatised Mr Wills as an alien because he was born in the adjacent county of Devonshire.

Below Supporters of Sir Randolf Baker about to leave Hinton St Mary to vote at the Sturminster Newton polling station in 1906. At the close of polling the local ballot-boxes would be conveyed to Sturminster Newton and the result announced early the next day, unless the poll had been so close that there needed to be a recount.

Crowds awaiting the declaration of the poll in the Market Square in Sturminster. The two-storey building to the left of the Swan was the Carpenters Arms public house.

Above A photographic postcard printed in celebration of Mr A W Wills' success for the Liberals in the North Dorset By-Election of 1905, taken after the declaration of the poll at Gillingham. Beside the driver sits Mr Lyell, MP for East Dorset, holding a card proclaiming the 909 majority by which Mr Wills had beaten the Conservative, Sir Randolf Baker. The Liberal vote was 4,239; the Conservatives vote 3,330.

Below Another triumph for the Liberals in 1906, with Mr Wills receiving 4,143 votes against Sir Randolf Baker's 3,508 for the Conservatives, giving the Liberals a slightly reduced majority of 645. Mr Wills is in the car on the left, the only one not wearing a hat.

It would appear that politicians have always had their every move recorded for posterity. Both photographs were taken on 6th May 1908.

Right The Liberal MP Mr Wills and his wife, Margery, at the opening of the Wesleyan Bazaar in Stalbridge.

Below Mr and Mrs Wills on their way to the Drill Hall in Station Road, Stalbridge.

NORTH DORSET ELECTION, 1910.

POLLING DAY:
WEDNESDAY, JAN. 19th,
From 8 a.m. to 8 p.m.

YOU VOTE AT—
BOYS' NATIONAL SCHOOL,
STURMINSTER NEWTON.

Your Register Number is **X 106**

You are earnestly requested to

VOTE FOR BAKER

by making a **X** on the Ballot Paper in the square
to the right of his name.

1	**BAKER**	**X**
2	WILLS	

DO NOT sign your name.
DO NOT write your initials.
DO NOT make any mark except a **X**
FOLD your Ballot Paper, and put it in the Box.
IF YOU spoil the Ballot Paper, ask for another.

Above The declaration of the poll at the Boy's National School in Penny Street, Sturminster Newton in January 1910.

Left A mock voting paper in January 1910, the first of two general elections that year during a period of political turmoil. The Liberal agent, Mr Beer, alleged malpractice against some people working for Conservative candidate Sir Randolf Baker. It was reported that they would go to the homes of voters with what appeared to be official ballot papers and ask them to place a cross alongside their preferred candidate. If they placed their cross beside the Liberal candidate they were told that they no longer needed to go to the poll as they had now voted. Sir Randolf took the seat held by A W Wills since 1905.

Below The Market Place during the declaration of the poll in 1910.

Photographed from the old Assembly Rooms over what is now Holebrooks butcher's, a crowd gathers in the Market Place to hear the Conservative candidate, Sir Randolph Baker, give his winning speech on 20th January 1910.

In Times of War

Town Crier Kevin Knapp leading the pipes and drums of the Wessex Highlanders up Church Street on Remembrance Sunday in 2014, which marked the 100th anniversary of the outbreak of World War I.

Above Troops marching through the Market Place during World War I. To the right, wagons belonging to Hall & Woodhouse.

Right Troops awaiting departure from Sturminster Newton station. *Inset* Charlie Stride holding his son (also called Charlie). He became a Colour Sergeant in the Dorsetshire Regiment and was a familiar figure in the area. He was a founding member of the Sturminster Newton Branch of the British Legion, and was at one time agent to the Rivers Estate. Charlie Stride was an accomplished photographer and many of his pictures appear in this book.

Below Soldiers of the Dorsetshire Regiment pose outside the Swan.

Above A sketch from a local autograph book by one of the RFA (Royal Field Artillery) troops when they were stationed in Sturminster during World War I.

Below Members of the Dorsetshire Regiment collecting for the Red Cross with Charlie Stride between the shafts. The photograph is thought to have been taken in Dorchester.

In 1915 the Guardians of the Sturminster Union Workhouse in Bath Road were asked to provide space in their building to set up a Red Cross Hospital. The Guardians gave up their boardroom for the purpose and it was taken over by members of the Voluntary Aid Attachments Nos 18 and 62 Dorset, many of whom appear in the photograph above. They looked after the NCOs and men of the 26th Divisional Ammunition Column, RFA, who were billeted in the neighbourhood at the time. The commandant of No 18 Dorset was A M Whatman, and A Charlesworth was commandant of No 62 Dorset; their quartermaster was F M Watts Silvester, and the medical officer looking after the men was Dr T H E Watts Silvester.

Right A studio photograph of one of the Red Cross workers. The name on the back refers to her simply as "Molly"; she does not appear in the group picture above.

Above An intriguing image of troops in the Market Place. The large wagons on the left appear to contain livestock while, to the right, groups of soldiers rest outside the Swan and the Carpenters Arms.

Right Excerpts from Sturminster Newton Parish Magazines of 1915 and 1917.

Below Members of the Royal Horse Artillery parading their animals in the Market Place. The archway in the background, which led to stables behind the Swan, is now the main entrance to Holebrooks butcher's shop. Cressey's Antique shop is to the right.

DECEMBER, 1915.

Special Notices.

Every Week-day Evensong at 7-30 p.m. with special prayers appointed for use in the Church at the present time (except Tuesdays at 7 p.m.)

Every day at noon the Church bell is tolled for the uplifting of all hearts in prayer on behalf of our Soldiers and Sailors and supplication for peace and victory.

1915 The Knitting Brigade. – The recent cold weather has made us at home feel the need for warmer clothing, and it should also remind us that the time has now come when our brave sailors and soldiers will also need all the warm woolen comforts that we can send them. Last winter a band of ladies met regularly to knit scarves, mittens, gloves, helmets, socks, etc., and, as a result of their labours, several hundred of these useful and necessary articles were sent abroad. The Knitting Brigade have already made arrangements to restart their useful work, but as wool is expensive, they will be very glad of any donations to help defray their expenses.

1917 War Savings Association. – The Secretary of our Branch, Mr F. G. Symonds, reports that he has sold 224 War Saving Certificates, and he hopes to bring the number up to 250 during the next fortnight. We must all help our Country to win this War by buying War Saving Certificates at once, or taking a War savings Card, and with the Sixpences saved, buy sixpenny War Savings Stamps. There are 31 squares on the card, and on each of those squares must be put a 6d War Savings Stamp. When the card is filled up it must exchanged for a War Savings Certificate, then get a fresh card and go on saving as before, do not wait to be asked, join at once ! Remember that the British Government's security for your money is the best in the World.

1917 Cultivation of Allotments. – A Strong Voluntary Committee has been formed to arrange for the Cultivation of the Allotments belonging to men who are serving their King and Country. A public meeting, which was well attended, was held in the Church Schools. If funds are forthcoming the Committee will, in cases of real need, provide artificial manure & lime. The idea is to organize and concentrate effort on securing a good potato crop. Mr. Tatman, Mr. Hanks, and Mr. Walters have shown special energy in starting "The Sturminster Newton Voluntary Allotment War Work Scheme."

Shop Talk, No. 8.

Above Members of the Dorsetshire Regiment local to the Sturminster Newton area in October 1914. *Back row from left* Jack Upshall, ?, J Ridout, Reg Cressey, ?, W Ridout.
Middle row from left W White, ?, "Natty" Cluett, Colour Sergeant Charlie Stride, A Hussey, H Collins. *Front row from left* ?, Ted Marsh, ?.

Above A well-posed photograph featuring members of the Dorsetshire Regiment. Standing left is Charlie Stride and on the right, smoking a pipe, is another local man Jack (John) Watts who used to work as a blacksmith and wheelwright for the Beales opposite the Bull Inn.

Above This poor quality but important image was taken on 24th September 1919 at the presentation of a German field gun and carriage to Shillingstone. The gun was "Captured in the Final Advance, September, 1918" and was "Presented by the War Office to the Parish of Shillingstone in recognition of its magnificent record in Voluntary Recruiting". During the period before compulsory service, Shillingstone sent more men per capita in response to the call to Colours than any other village in Great Britain.

Below Moving forward to the early days of World War II, the same field gun is to the left of the picture – but not for much longer. When the call came for scrap metal, Shillingstone once again proved its worth and gave up its precious gun to be melted down for the war effort.

Above Members of Lydlinch Home Guard. *Back from left* Harold Hyde, Jack Hannam, Charlie Cluett, Jim Hawkins, Reg Rendell, Harold Frizzle, George Brown, Gordon Lane.
Middle from left John Cluett, Jim Cluett, Alfred Lane, Arthur Mowlem, Morris Lane, Owen Stainer, Jack Mogg, Bob Tuffin. *Front from left* Raymond Saunders, George Frizzle, Harold Cluett, George Thorne and Percy Kirby.

Above and *below* The Two Fords steel bridge, on the A357 between Bagber and Lydlinch, was built by Canadian army engineers in 1942. Early in World War II there were already outline plans for the D-Day invasion and a key element of these was the swift and efficient movement of troops. The original stone bridge over the River Lydden was deemed too weak to carry the weight of heavy equipment, and so this "temporary" double-truss Callender-Hamilton bridge was constructed. It is still going strong today, albeit with a bit of attention from time to time.

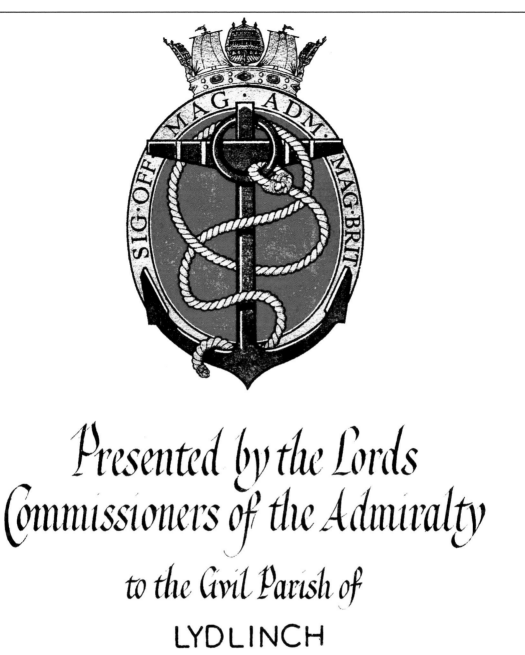

Presented by the Lords
Commissioners of the Admiralty

to the Civil Parish of

LYDLINCH

to commemorate the adoption of

H.M.S. L.23

during Warship Week — — FEBRUARY, 1942

Although a handsome and ornate shield was presented to Sturminster Rural District Council, additional framed certificates, like the one above, were presented to the outlying Civic Parishes in recognition of their contribution during Warship Week in February 1942.

Above The names of these evacuees to Sturminster during WW2, outside the Summer House at Hinton St Mary, were not known when the photograph was previously published. Now, however, it has been possible to identify some of them. *Descending from top left* Sylvia Eden, Leah Clarke, Dorothy Overton, Doris Rolfe, Marjorie Crawford (Maid of Honour), Irene Robinson, Mary Gent, ?, ?, Doris Mitchell, Irene Burnage, Doreen Carter, ?.

Above Another photograph of the evacuees, taken at Sturminster Bridge. Among those on the bridge are Dorothy Overton (fourth from left) and Doris Rolfe, Sylvia Eden, Irene Burnage (third, second and first from right). In the foreground are Betty Cater (picking flowers), Eileen Kimble, Irene Robinson and Doris Nayler.

Above This World War II group photograph, posed in front of the Market Cross in Sturminster, has caused much speculation over the years. So far, nobody has been able to identify the men or the story behind the photo. To add to the mystery, many of them are wearing Dorsetshire Regiment cap badges, but a number of them are not. The consensus is that they are possibly a POW (Prisoner of War) escort detail complete with outriders.

Below Italian POW's working in Piddles Wood. They would be brought in on a daily basis to do jobs such as felling trees and sawing timber. They probably came from a POW camp that was situated nearby at Motcombe.

Above Peggy Hatcher of the Women's Land Army, sitting on the wing of one of the Ministry of Agriculture and Fisheries vans that were used to transport the girls to the various farms where they worked.

Left Posing against a hayrick, other members of the Land Army; they were billeted at Manston.

Above The harvesting crew at Home Farm, Fifehead Neville, beside a corn thrasher. *From left* Absalom Fields, Land Army girl, Kath Trowbridge, Phil Adams, two more Land Army girls, Sidney Trowbridge, Arthur Goddard, Mr Warr's son, Mr May, Mr Pitman, Mr Griffin, Hilda Pitman. The two girls at the front are *left* Vera Griffin and Violet Griffin.

The Wings for Victory parade in Sturminster Newton on
30th May 1943. Members of the RAF, RCAF, RAAF, WAAF
and ATC travelled up from Bournemouth, where they were
stationed, to attend the Drumhead Service at 3pm in the
Recreation Ground.

At one point a flypast was announced over the loudspeaker
and, with the weather remaining fine, everyone was thrilled to
watch a single aeroplane perform its flying routine.

After the service the participants were treated to an
excellent buffet. Food was rationed and the members of the
armed services were surprised and grateful for the meal as it
was obvious that the inhabitants of Sturminster had sacrificed
some of their own rations to lay on the spread.

No chapter about the war years in Sturminster would be complete without mentioning the Sturminster Newton Home Guard. The three photographs on these two pages are a Who's Who of Sturminster family names. They show, above and below, the two squads that formed the local Home Guard and, on the right, the "officers of rank".

Above, back row from left Gordon Phillips, Norman "Ginger" Short, Jim Downes, Stan Clarke (runner), Vic Lewis (runner), Jim Crew, Vic Cross, Arthur Score, P Hart, H Walker.
Middle row from left Bert Deverill, Fred Elkins, Norkus Rose, Alfie Cluett, Hector Beale, Bob Hitt (armourer), Bob Spencer, Ken Doggrell.
Front row from left Charlie Drake, Tom Gray, S Gray, P Hillier, P L Goddard, Merv Hatcher, T Burt, Victor White.

Above, back row from left Wilf Clarke, L G Tippetts, G Hunt, Arthur Warren, Bert Inkpen, C Hunt, Frank Cowley, T Pratt, E Curtis.
Middle row from left Reg Rose, Walt Senior, Jim Chambers, Alec Knott, Leonard Inkpen, J "Mousey" Harris, Harry Crew, Ray Beale, Percy Dennis.
Front row from left Percy Rose, Jim Duffett, Harry Matthews, Jack Duffett, Wally Selby, Jim Hatcher, Bob Duffett.

Above The "officers of rank" of the Sturminster Newton Home Guard.
Back row from left Walt Senior, R "Bovril" Inkpen, Max Beale, Harry Crew, Ray Beale, Ken Doggrell
Middle row from left Morris Stacey, J "Mousey" Harris, Leonard Inkpen, G C Sloane Stanley, Jesse Short, Bert Hill, Hector Beale, Norkus Rose
Front row from left Cyril Score, Jim Chambers, Alfie Cluett, T H Corbin, Alec Knott, Bob Hitt (armourer)

Right Three members of the Home Guard: *from left* "Mack" Tite, whose mother used to own Drake's shop on the corner of Station Road; Harold Clarke, who was at one time the Commander in Chief of the Home Guard; and Stan Clarke.

The headquarters of the Home Guard was opposite the White Hart. It was said that if the building ever received a direct hit or had been bombed, there was enough explosive stored on the premises to blow up most of Stur.

War also meant a sudden influx of new faces, which was obviously as interesting to the troops as it was to the locals. *Above* Taken at Hinton St Mary, the young ladies at the front are *from left* D Stockley, P Strong (née Turk), M Inkpen (née Bennett), P Hall (née Curtis), D Wines, J Metcalf (née Lemon). The troops are believed to be from the Surrey and Sussex Yeomanry.

Below Later in the war the Americans came to Sturminster. Taken in 1944 down by the river Stour, the three Americans are *from left* Corporal Douglas Greenfield, Sergeant Ewell Blaylock and Technician 4th Grade Sergeant Eddie Strebig. The young ladies are *from left* Muriel Ware, Betty Tite and Marion Lewis.

Above Members of 808 Naval Air Squadron taken at Henstridge Airfield (HMS Dipper) in 1944. *Back row from left* L Martin, M L Heath, J F Rankin, P A Sherry, B C White *Front row from left* W D Hughes, A W Bradley, F Waldie, D H Jenkins, G T Cooper, S K Radnor, N J Bowen, A A Cogill, D R Hill

At the time of this photograph, the members of 808 Squadron were facing an uncertain future. They had arrived at Henstridge early in March to sharpen up their flying and, in particular, their low flying and attacking skills. During this period the skies above the Blackmore Vale would have been positively buzzing with aircraft – never before had so many planes been based at Henstridge at any one time. However, this intense activity was to be short lived; by the end of March the wing was moved back to Lee-on-Solent in preparation for D-Day.

Above Members of the Sturminster Newton Royal Observer Corp at Rixon in September 1944. *Back row standing from left* Archie Hussey, Billy Wills, Frank Painter, Reg Cressey, George Bastable, Claude Teed, Cyril Hallett, Sidney Guy, Arthur Barnett, Jack (Jim) Hindley *Front row sitting from left* Roy Hatcher, Cyril Miles, Sexton Blake, Joe Horder, Ernest Miller, Fred Gray, Bert Duffett.

The chapter ends on a poignant note. *Above* A photograph only recently come to light shows Charles Trowbridge, a smallholder and thatcher from Okeford Fitzpaine, standing beside the tail section of a downed German Heinkel 111 plane in which all the crew lost their lives. *Below from left* Colonel William Douglas Whatman, who set up the Sturminster Newton Branch of the Royal British Legion to help men returning home from World War I; John Inkpen from Shillingstone who, besides wearing his own medals, wears those of his three sons killed in the Great War; and Charlie Stride, who lost his son in World War II.

Hinton St Mary

The view from Higher Cross from outside the White Horse public house towards Lower Cross
where the main Marnhull Road is today. The man sitting on the wall is Enos Keniston.

Above and *below* Cutt Mill in happier times, in the 1980s. Even the interior of the mill, as can be seen below, was in an incredibly good state of repair, which makes the fire that devastated the building in 2003 all the more tragic.

Above Cutt Mill circa 1920. Ivor Hunt (miller), left; standing in the cart is Herbert Hunt (miller and farmer); sitting is Claude Hunt (who also became a miller and farmer), holding a pike. Ivor and Herbert are carrying strings of eels.

Below Two views of Cutt Mill in 1950 showing the difference in water levels when it floods.

Above Tiddles showing remarkable restraint confronted with the day's catch at Cutt Mill.

Below Claude Hunt, who shared the miller's job at Cutt Mill with his brother Gordon, in the kitchen of the miller's cottage. Some scenes for the TV drama *Fair Stood the Wind for France* are said to have been shot in this kitchen and parts of the building altered for the production.

Above Hinton St Mary School, taken circa 1913 outside St Peter's Church.
Back row from left Miss Ida Rose, Miss Rachel Kiddle. Miss Kiddle was head teacher from 1911 to 1915; she arrived at Hinton St Mary by bicycle on 1st April 1911 and asked directions from a local blacksmith, Walter White; she later married him.
Third row from left ?, ?, ?, ?, ?, Albert King, Ada Hoddinot, Nelly or Lily Maidment, ?, ?, ?, ?, Dorothy Rose, Edith Warren, ?, ?
Second row from left Fred Whitlock, Queenie Whitlock, Nelly Whitlock, Rebecca Chinn, ?, Teresa Hunt, Olive Hoddinott, Ruth Chinn, ?, ?, Harold Maidment, Hermi White, Hilda Dennis, Gwenie Rose, Mabel Pedder
Front from left ?, ? Balls, ? Balls, ?, George Rose, ?, Gladys Warren, Percival Lewis, Patty Chinn, ?, ?.

Below The classroom at Hinton St Mary School.

Above An irresistible image despite the damage: George Bastable and Jim Innes in front of the gates to the Manor House at Hinton, wearing their green jackets reserved for special occasions, this one being the 1945 Wessex Festival of Music.

Below A general view of the ancient Manor House, home of the Pitt-Rivers family.

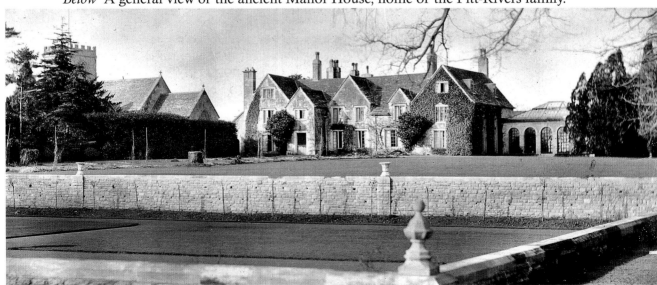

Above This is believed to be Brigadier-General Robert and Lady Flora Poore, at one time tenants in the area, with the Hinton St Mary junior cricket team. The General was an excellent cricketer – in 1923, when 57 years old, he hit three consecutive centuries during a tour of the MCC in the West Country – and he took an interest in encouraging youngsters to play the game. That Hinton had such a good team for so many years was probably due in no small part to his enthusiasm and the skills he passed on.

Below The magnificent Tithe Barn in 2010.

Above and *below* On Thursday 27th August 1908 there was a Grand Fête and Baby Show in the gardens of the Manor House. It was opened at 12.30pm by Princess Anne of Lowenstein-Wertheim. Entertainments included old English country dances, a bazaar, rifle shooting and dancing to the Sturminster Town and Military Bands; in the evening the lawns were illuminated with fairy lights. The prize for the finest and healthiest baby was won by Mrs Caines of Sturminster Newton. The fête was held at the Manor House because Mrs Pitt-Rivers was the originator of the St Mary's Nursing Association – St Mary's Nursing Home was in Sturminster Newton – the intended beneficiary of the profits.

Six years later, the British born princess was the first woman to be flown across the English Channel (she had several other records to her name). In 1927, at the age of 63, she was a passenger on an attempt at the first transatlantic east-to-west flight. The plane disappeared without trace and was assumed to have gone down somewhere off Newfoundland.

Above Members of the Hinton St Mary Church of England Temperance Society on an outing in 1907.

Left Richard Moore, for many years clerk at St Peter's Church in Hinton. It is thought that the lectern in the church is a memorial to him.

Right A view of St Peter's Church in the early 1900s.

Above Pupils of Hinton St Mary School in 1937, photographed in the School Yard.
Back row from left Derek Crew, Jack Turk, Peter Chant, Harold Rose, Pam Turk, Joyce Deverill, Vera Bastable. *Front row from left* Roma Burt, Ruth Reed, Betty Derk, Percy Bastable, Bennie (Benita) King, John Lambert, Grenville Lambert.

The head teacher was Mrs Noakes, and there was one other teacher, Miss Rose. It was said to have been a very happy school, which gave its pupils a good grounding in general education. At one time there were up to 70 children, until the 11 to 14-year-olds were required to attend school in Sturminster Newton.

Below Pupils of Hinton School performing the Scarf Dance.

Above Miss Guest's Hunt outside the White Horse. The hunt was an offshoot of the Blackmore Vale Hunt. Miss Guest, left riding side-saddle, came from Inwood, the daughter of Merthyr Guest, who had been the Master of the Blackmore Vale Hunt for 16 years. In 1914, at the invitation of the Committee, she started hunting with her private pack.

Below Mr and Mrs Strong, landlord and landlady of the White Horse for many years.

Above To the left is the White Horse and on the right, the old pond that was filled in in 1956.

Right No Health and Safety regulations to observe, Samuel Rose, left, with Enos Keniston sharpening a reap hook on a hand-operated grinding wheel.

Below Members of the Chinn family outside Twinwood Farm in 1913. Note the towering English Elm trees in the background.

Above Outside Lindens in Goughs Close, Sturminster Newton, in 1916, Mrs Beatrice Crew and Mrs Olga Drew delivering bread. The horse's name was Fan and the cart belonged to Joseph King, a baker in Hinton St Mary during the late 1800s and early 1900s.

Around the same time there was a grocer and baker in Hinton St Mary, Mr Allen, who also delivered bread in Sturminster Newton using a covered cart pulled by a large white horse. One of his deliveries was at Mr Cressey's shop, now Holebrooks, in the Market Place. The front entrance to Cressey's had a very large door knocker which the horse would grip with its mouth and bang loudly until Mrs Cressey answered the door.

Below Later, in the 1920s, Mr Allen used a motorcycle to make some of his deliveries with this sidecar attachment to carry the bread.

Above Another interesting but slightly damaged photograph offers an early glimpse of Turk's garage on the main road at Hinton St Mary.

Below Taken in the early 1900s, this gloriously rural dwelling is in fact Hinton St Mary's Post Office. In 1903 the sub-postmaster was Enos Keniston, here standing behind the gate. Letters came through the sorting office at Sturminster arriving at 6.40am and 12 noon and were dispatched at 10.30am and 6.10pm. On Sunday, letters arrived at 6.40am and were dispatched at 6.10pm. Postal Orders were also issued and paid here.

Hinton St Mary was the site of an important find in 1963 when a remarkably well-preserved Romano-British mosaic floor was discovered on the land of blacksmith John White.
Above An aerial view of experts examining the Hinton Mosaic, believed to include one of the earliest depictions of Christ in Britain. The site was excavated in 1965 and the mosaic lifted and transferred to the British Museum for preservation and display.

Left Hinton blacksmiths William White and his son Walter White c. 1905.

Right Blacksmith Walter White and Arthur Sturgess display their handiwork, a chandelier thought to have been made for the Tythe Barn at Hinton. In the background is Bill Holly, the son of a neighbour.

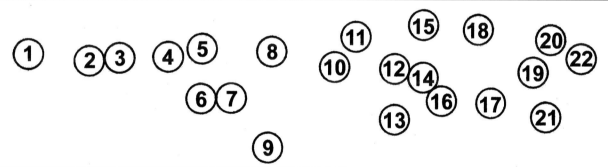

May Day Celebrations at Hinton St Mary in May 1958.
The photograph was taken outside the front of the school.

Key to numbers:
1 Stephen Bartlett, 2 Charmain Taunton, 3 Shirley Martin,
4 Shirley Steine, 5 Richard Rose, 6 Sheila Barter,
7 Geoffrey Lewis, 8 Sandra Barter, 9 Clive Siviter,
10 Eileen Innes, 11 Tony Dawe, 12 Marilyn Dallimore,
13 Sandra hodge, 14 Dennis Martin, 15 Colin Siviter,
16 Olive Douch, 17 Valerie Snook, 18 Tony Taunton,
19 Richard Notley, 20 Robert Guy, 21 Sheena Guy,
22 Noreen Martin.

Right Mr Dawe, the driver of the tractor and trailer,
who transported the children around the village.

Above The main road entering Hinton St Mary from Sturminster, taken in 1898, with Bob Moore in the foreground. The old forge is in the background. The gateway to the left apparently led to the place where many of the villagers used to draw their water.

Below The main road leading out of Hinton towards Marnhull.

Around and About

A young Ian Kendall of Marnhull standing beside the signpost at Walton Elm – the perfect image to introduce this chapter, which dips into the archives to offer a selection of photographs from around the area that might otherwise have remained unseen. Sturminster Newton has always been as much about the people and places around it as about the town itself.

Above Members of the Rose family in the early 1900s camping at Fiddleford, a popular camping site at the time. Note the guns leaning against the tent at back left along with, presumably, the next meal hanging up beside them. People would load up a boat with tents, cooking equipment and provisions, plus their guns, and set off downstream until they found a suitable spot – after asking permission from the land owner of course.

Above Another of those mystery photographs. It is stamped A R Hallett of Sturminster Newton and dates from before World War I. The plane has landed in a field somewhere in or around the town but the story behind the photo is unknown. "EWEN" on the tail might refer to the Scottish aviator William Hugh Ewen, who was awarded an Aviators Certificate by the Royal Aero Club on 14th February 1911.

Above The Crown Inn at Ibberton, centre background, in the early 1900s; it was originally called the New Inn. Part of the building dates back to the 16th century and still retains many original features such as a bread oven, inglenook fireplace and flagstone floor. The local postman poses in the foreground.

Below left Miss Wells, who was once the headmistress of Ibberton School. She was appointed by the Reverend Wix, and the photograph is thought to have been taken sometime before 1899.

Below right Bert Courage from Ibberton in the 1930s.

Above Members of the Clarke family and friends in front of Fifehead Neville Mill where Frank Clarke, front centre of group, was the miller for many years. In days gone by the mill had four or five carthorses along with a pony and trap for deliveries and collections. If you walked around the buildings at night with a hurricane lamp, you would be greeted by the reflection of hundreds of twinkling rodent eyes.

Above The staff at Prideaux's Milk Factory in Kings Stag circa 1950. The factory made cheese and "Dorsella", a full cream milk food specially prepared from pure clean milk.
Back row from left Archie Mogg, ?, Pat Watts, Cissy King, Reuben Ricketts, Ruth Ricketts, Stella Phillips, ? Barter, Tom Barter. *Front row from left* Sylvia Meaden, Betty Ford, Heather Trevett, Betty Moore, Dennis Pope (manager), Jean Trevett, Ann Frizell, ? King.

Above left The Singing Kettle tearoom, previously the Rose and Crown pub, used to be on the A357 at Bagber. It was a popular meeting place for all ages.

Above right Around 1961 the building to the right of the Singing Kettle was demolished and the garage premises in this photograph were built by the then garage owner Mr L Dodson. Today the site is the business premises of C J Cox Ltd.

Above Bagber school children proudly wearing their good attendance medals. Some of them would have taken part in the Dorset Choral Association's Competitive Musical Festival, which the school regularly entered in the Small Villages section. The shield is believed to have been won at one of these competitions. Bagber School had around 50 pupils in the early 1920s. The mistress, who had a residence at the school, was a Miss M A Gardiner but it is not known if she is either of the adults in the photograph.

Above If you were travelling along the A357 through Lydlinch towards Sturminster Newton 100 years ago this would have been the view along the main road. The Three Boars Heads public house, later called the Deer Park, was built in the late 18th century and, although no longer a pub, the building remains. The position of the original route was slightly south of today's road and was said to be so narrow that two packhorses could not pass by each other. Because of this, a horn was hung at either end of the stretch: a horseman entering would blow a warning to any rider coming from the other direction.

Below A view of the old Lydlinch Post Office, now closed, which also stood beside the A357.

Above The Stalbridge Players in "The Old Women in the Shoe" held in the old Hut in 1955. For the production Margaret Walter had asked for a fountain, but it wasn't until the dress rehearsal that she realised the back stage boys had managed to fulfil her request. Unfortunately, they then had to keep pumping water by hand throughout the entire scene every evening and probably wished that they'd never engineered it at all. The *Western Gazette* reported that Dick Meader's work in managing to produce a fountain had been "spectacular".

Above Taken in December 1982, this is the earliest known photograph of the *Blackmore Vale Magazine* staff based in Stalbridge. *From left* Sven Thomas, Mary ?, Ingrid Chalcraft, Alan Chalcraft, in front of him Enid holding Gillie the dog, Fran Watts on the bike, and Ray ?. When Alan and Ingrid took over the magazine in 1978 it was a small eight-page foldout, but it grew into the weekly publication we know today.

Above This Toll House used to stand on the Dorset and Somerset boundary, where the A357 crosses Landshire Lane between Stalbridge and Henstridge. Anyone passing the Toll Gate at this point would have been greeted by an old man on crutches demanding 4½d (four and a half old pence) for a traveller and horse and slightly less for a mule or donkey.

Right A poster advertising a sale of the Tolls generated by the Vale of Blackmoor Turnpike Roads in 1858.

Below This peaceful rural scene is today the busy junction at the traffic lights of the A357 and A30 at Henstridge. The building to the left is the Virginia Ash, then known as the Old Ash and the Virginia Hotel, and to the right are the old reading rooms. The upstairs of this building used to be the youth club and downstairs was an area where social events were held.

VALE OF BLACKMOOR
TURNPIKE ROADS.

Notice is hereby given,

THAT THE

TOLLS

Arising at the undermentioned Toll Gates,
on the Vale of Blackmoor Turnpike Roads, will be

LET BY AUCTION,

TO THE BEST BIDDER,

On TUESDAY, NOVEMBER 9th, 1858,

At the House of MR. HUTCHINGS, known by the name of the
CROWN INN, in Sturminster Newton Castle, between the
hours of 12 at Noon, and 2 o'clock in the Afternoon,

For One Year,

In the manner directed by the Acts of Parliament in that behalf, and subject to such Conditions as
will be then produced ; and will be put up either in one Lot, or in the undermentioned, or such other
Lots, and at such sums, as the Trustees present shall think proper,—which Tolls were Let for, or
produced, the last year as follows :—

	£	s.	d.		£	s.	d.
Enford, Shillingston, and New-Cross Gates	296	0	0	Yewstock Gate	111	0	0
				Whitepost Gates	68	0	0
Newton and Bagber Gates	161	0	0	Milton and Gillingham Gates, and Pern's Mill and Bay Lane Gates	272	0	0
Landshire Lane & Horsington Gates	252	0	0				
Walbridge Gates	71	10	0				

ABOVE THE EXPENSES OF COLLECTING THE SAME.

The Tolls at all the Gates will be Let from the 31st. day of December, 1858, to the 31st. day of December, 1859.

Whoever happens to be the best Bidder, will be required to pay One Month's Rent in advance, and
at the same time give Security, with two sufficient Sureties, to the satisfaction of the Trustees of
the said Turnpike Roads, for payment of the Rents at which such Tolls shall be Let, Monthly, or in
such other proportions as they shall direct ; and the Persons proposed as Sureties must either attend
personally at the time of Letting the said Tolls, or send an undertaking in writing under their hands
that they will become Sureties, otherwise the Letting will be void, and the Tolls will be put up again
immediately, and no Person will be allowed to bid, unless he or she shall previously make a Deposit of
such a sum, as shall be determined on by the Trustees at the time of Letting ; which sum will in case
such Person shall happen to be the best Bidder, be retained by the Treasurer in part of the Rent so to
be paid in advance as aforesaid.

BY ORDER OF THE TRUSTEES.

Dated the 28th. of September, 1858.   **DASHWOOD & SON, Clerks.**

W. TRITE, PRINTER, STURMINSTER.

These two pages give an impression of what life was like above and below stairs in the late 1800s. The photographs on both pages were taken at Nash Court in Marnhull.

Above A group picture of the staff at Nash Court, and *below* scrubbing the front doorstep.

Right The main image is a general view of Nash Court; *inset top left* Captain Edwin Greenwood Hardy, who lived at Nash Court with *inset top right* his wife Mary.

Above The Crown Hotel in Marnhull, which appears in Thomas Hardy's *Tess of the D'Urbervilles* as the Pure Drop Inn.

Above A personal favourite, this 1903 photograph shows the frontage of Edward Jason Rawles' boot and shoe shop in Marnhull, with photogenic dog.

Above The wonderful sight of a waterwheel in full flow at King's Mill, Marnhull in the early 1900s. George Hatcher, who lived at King's Mill in about 1850, and Robert Burge from Stalbridge, used to send their cattle to London by road. They would begin moving the herd on Sunday evening and would reach Smithfield on Wednesday evening.

Above The Plough Inn at Manston when Arthur Courage was the licensee. This photograph dates from around 1903. The sign on the front reads: "Plough Inn. Matthews & Co's Noted Dorset Ales Wines & Spirits".

Above The Manston Tug of War Team in the mid-1970s. *Back row from left* Ken Wilson (coach), Henry Card, Jimmy Loader, Keith Murphy, R Walters, John Starkey, Martyn Lewis, Richard Eavis, George Woodsford (Weymouth AAA rep), John Drew. *Front row from left* Terry Morgan, Paul Yeatman, Martin Yeatman, Damion Bittner, Peter Edlin

Above Staff and pupils at Manston School in June 1972. *Back row from left* Mrs Russell, Mrs Jackson, Roger Read, Ian Farnborough, Lynette Dyke, Ellen Tucker, Alison Chisell, Della Read, Stephanie Hunt, Mary Ann Short, Sue Cooke, Rosalind Danoris, John Dunning, Mrs Hunt and Mrs Short. *Middle row from left* Rodney Tucker, Linda Read, Ros Candy, Andrew Chisell, Sandra Conway, Serena Christopher, Chris Netherway, Julie Dunning, Steve Short, Andrew Danoris. *Front row from left* Alan Tucker, Colin Read, Amanda Lewis, Jane Farnborough, Robert Plumber, Philip Short, Jane Netherbury, Louanne Gibson, Michelle Hunt, Heidi Gibson, Sarah Netherway.

Above Fiddleford 1951, Fred Yeatman driving the wagon accompanied by a young Sidney Rose. This image was used on the front cover of local author Olive Knott's story collection *Tales of Dorset* published in 1985.

Above The centre of Child Okeford in the early 1900s with the Baker's Arms on the right. To its left is Mr Turner's butcher's shop. At one time he had two parrots in cages outside the shop. As the school children walked by they tried to teach the parrots to talk. The children were so successful, the parrots ended up learning words that Mr Turner had never bargained for, so the birds were taken inside. Mr Turner himself was not averse to making the odd comment that would raise a few eyebrows today. On greeting a man recently returned from honeymoon, Mr Turner remarked that his new wife was "a damned good heifer".

Above and *below* Shroton Fair at the beginning of the last century. The fair was held on 25th and 26th September, its main purpose being the buying and selling of horses, cattle and produce. In the evening the fair would be illuminated by naphtha flares, a highly volatile and flammable liquid which would be considered extremely dangerous today. The attractions seen in the photographs, including the merry-go-round below, would of course all have been powered by steam.

Right A bad day for a lorry driver on Durweston Bridge. When he was finally rescued the driver passed out from sheer fright – and one can quite see why. The accident happened in the late 1920s; initially there were fears that the River Stour would be polluted by the chemicals the lorry was transporting.

Above This pretty rural scene is actually the main road through Shillingstone circa 1900. The New Ox Inn is on the right. In 1959 when the pub closed it became the Good Earth tea shop. The thatched cottages next to it have long since been demolished. This colourful postcard is an another excellent example of hand-tinted photographs.

Below A family group from Shillingstone: on the left, Una Snook pulls a cart containing her brothers and sister; *from left* Derek Snook, Pam Snook (later Cole) holding baby Trevor Snook, Raymond Snook and Maurice Snook and, centre, Sport the dog.

Above Members of the Shillingstone Girl Guides in 1944/45. *Back row from left* Pam Brown, Pam Read, Beryl Baker, Isobel Amey, Betty Brown, Pam Snook, Joan Pope, Irene Patasric. *Front row from left* Hilary Burgore, Sheila Amey and Mrs Jarrett.

Above Another view of the New Ox Inn in Shillingstone. To the left, in a white apron, is Robert (Bob) Stone, the landlord. He was also the local carpenter and undertaker.

The New Inn in Okeford Fitzpaine was a very small and intimate pub that had no bar as such. Customers would go up to a stable door in the room to order their drinks.

A chair was placed either side of a large open fire beside which a saucepan hung on the wall. If you felt your beer was too cold, you could pour it into the saucepan and warm it over the fire before returning it to your glass.

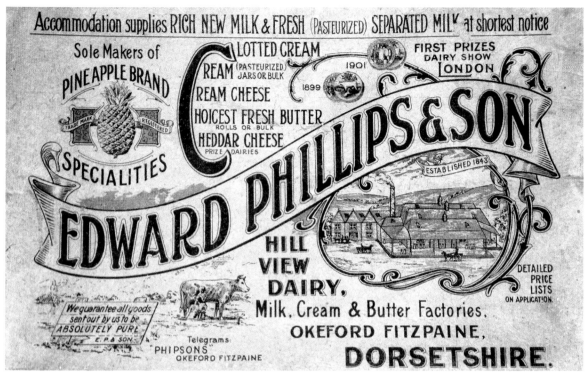

Above The design on the front of an Edward Phillips & Son packaging case. This rare survivor is in Sturminster Newton Museum's collection. Edward Phillips & Son, established in 1843 at Hillview Dairies in Okeford Fitzpaine, was one of the many small independent dairies in the area. The business survived into the 1970s when it became part of Webb's Country Foods.

Below An interesting image from the early 1900s showing a steam-powered milk collection and delivery wagon. The two men are thought to be Mr Hustings, left, and George Oliver. When the machine was first driven from Ibberton to Woolland, the entire village of Ibberton turned out to see it, not because it was something new and exciting but because everyone was convinced that a small bridge along the route would collapse beneath its weight. Fortunately both bridge and machine survived unscathed.

A striking image to end this book. It is believed to have been taken at the beginning of the 1900s somewhere in or around Hinton St Mary. There is no record of who the man was, but it would be fair to say that life had not been easy for him. It is tempting to look at old photographs through rose-tinted spectacles, but this photograph is a reminder of the hardships endured by many in an area beset by rural poverty.